The Stop Smoking Book

Margaret Kraker McKean

Illustrations by Wendell Dowling

Impact 🕮 **Publishers**
Post Office Box 1094
San Luis Obispo, California 93406

The Library of Congress has cataloged the first printing of this title as follows.

McKean, Margaret.
    The stop smoking book / Margaret McKean; illustrations by Wendell Dowling. — San Luis Obispo, Calif.: Impact Publishers, c1976.

    112p.: ill.; 21 cm.
    ISBN 0-915166-36-4: $2.95

    1. Cigarette habit. 2. Smoking.   I. Title.
HV5740.M32   616.86'506—dc19   76-26302
                                          MARC

Library of Congress   77[r84]rev

Printed in the United States of America

Published by *Impact* 🐚 *Publishers*
POST OFFICE BOX 1094
SAN LUIS OBISPO, CALIFORNIA 93406

Dedication

. . . . to stop smoking and write a book. . . .
Mac said I should, could and would.
Betty said I could.
Phyllis said I would.
Toni, Mike, Molly, Pat, Paul, Jamie and Kevin said my privilege of being their mother qualifies me for anything.
But the proudest of all, of both accomplishments, would be my parents.

Publisher's Note

When we first published this excellent book in 1976, Maggie McKean was very much alive, vital, and brimming with enthusiasm to share her success: she had taught herself not to smoke.

Nine thousand copies were sold of the first edition – thanks in part to Maggie's unceasing efforts on behalf of the cause to which she was so deeply committed. When we let the book go out of print in 1980, it was with the greatest reluctance and regret.

Although she had successfully avoided cigarettes for several years, Maggie's 30-year habit caught up with her; cancer took her life in 1983.

We think the time and the momentum are right to bring back Maggie's book. Less than 30% of the U.S. population now smokes. And millions of those who do say they want to quit.

Margaret McKean is unique among authors of Impact Publishers books. All the others are written by professionals with graduate degrees and experience in the human services. This book is the single exception to that policy because I know of no professional, no hospital, no organization with a more effective approach to helping smokers who want to quit. The reason is simple: Margaret McKean knew what it means to be a dedicated smoker, and she knew how tough it is to stop. She acknowledged her own addiction to cigarettes, and cared enough about her fellow addicts to offer them support and honest help, instead of condemnation.

Few of us with professional credentials in psychology, counseling, or medicine – despite our years of practiced empathy with clients – can offer the understanding which Maggie shares in this book. It is self-help in the best sense, and it was written by a "qualified professional."

Robert E. Alberti, Ph.D.
Publisher

An Acknowledgement

Acknowledgements prefacing a book are made usually to people who proof-read and type. And to people who encourage. The people who proof-read and typed are important enough to me to have been paid for their work.

You people who encourage me are all around me. I recognize you but I don't know your names. I see your faces. I see you in the coffee shops, at the bus stops, at work, at the theatre, at school, at church, at the kids' baseball games, at grown-ups' ballgames, at club meetings, at the beach, at parties, in the restrooms, in your kitchens, in your cars.

You're all so wonderfully different, yet you have this one alikeness—the cigarette stuck in your face or between your fingers. I know why you're stuck with them. I know the need. I am very like you except that I'm learning not to need the cigarette in my face or fingers. Probably you are too, or you are thinking about not needing.

Maybe you discovered, as I have, what it is that keeps us needing.

It's fear. It's fear that it's going to hurt not to smoke; fear that we'll lose a close, best friend—cigarettes—if we don't light up; fear that we'll be somewhat paralyzed—malfunction physically or emotionally—without cigarettes; and finally, the big fear, that if we try to learn to not need cigarettes, we'll fail.

Fail. How appalling to consider! That we might fail. Unthinkable. We are obsessed with winning. Why risk being a failure? Better to keep on lighting up even though the little lights from a cigarette's tip can't brighten the places where we keep our fears. There are so many of us who keep setting up smoke screens so that our fears won't show.

There are 52 million cigarette smokers in the United States and 40 million of them want to stop smoking. Statisticians say that. Now how a statistician learned that—when I wouldn't admit even to my husband and other best friends that I wanted to stop smoking—I'll never know.

But even if the surveys are 90 per cent wrong, it means that there are still a bunch of us, five million or 40 million, who want to learn not to need. The five million are represented in my life by people who say to me "You're learning. A smoking furnace like you and you're learning!" and by more of you whom I see in the shops, in the restaurants, in your cars, clutching your burning pacifiers and looking joyless. You are why I write this. You are my encouragement. I acknowledge it and thank you.

About this Book — which is OUR Book

Dear people,
There are words about
25 WAYS
in this book to help unhook
you from nicotine.
But the most compelling WAY, the best WAY, the good-for-you WAY and the forever WAY,
will be found and formed
by you
because you are choosing to be free.
This book does not say you have to take up WRITING when you put down smoking. It doesn't say you should put down smoking. It says you have a CHOICE.

Sometimes it helps to WRITE about what's happening to you as you make the choice to get unhooked from cigarettes, and as you steadily do it. (You'll find some blank pages in the back of OUR book.)

> "Writing about it" can be "talking about it"
>> to your best friend,
>> to a tape-recorder,
>> to a letter, to a good friend.

It is important to make statements. When no one else seems to care to hear the statements you are making about this hard choice, this book will care.

Or maybe you'd like to write in diary form—:

> Tuesday: "Today I chose not to smoke during my coffee break and that choice made me feel good because........"

> Wednesday: "Today I realized that nobody can make me stop smoking. Only I can do that for me, so........"

Don't worry about your spelling or grammar. Your book is about your feelings. Feelings don't spell.

> Just take my WAYS, and add to them your WAYS,
>> to unhook you from nicotine.
> You can CHOOSE not to smoke.
> For whatever reasons you CHOOSE,
>> you will be able to look back
>>> LIBERATED
>>> FREE
>>> JOYOUS
> because you let cigarettes go. You just let them go.
>> And they let go of you.

Carry this book with you as you go. Use your you-power and these words to be stronger than nicotine.

> LOVE yourself enough
>> to choose not to smoke,
>>> my love,

Maggie McKean

Forward and Onward

People say Reynolds Tobacco Company stock went down 15 points when I had gone a day without a cigarette.

The stock market and my friends all took nose dives when five days went by and still I hadn't lit up. Nobody expected I'd last an hour without a cigarette.

Even my family, especially my family, couldn't believe my announcement—"I choose not to smoke. . ."

I am a smoker's smoker. A cigarette has been an extension of my fingers for 30 years. I smoked through lumbar pneumonia, and right up to the door of the delivery room when my babies were being born. I smoked next to signs that said "no smoking" and occasionally in church. I smoked when my smoke made everybody else sick.

I smoked for all reasons—because I was working, because I was resting; because I was happy, because I was unhappy; because I was tense, because I was relaxed; because I was worried; because I wasn't.

I have spent my last 50¢ for cigarettes when we were out of milk, and borrowed milk from my neighbors.

Cigarettes are to me instant gratification, there for the striking of a match, the click of a lighter.

I have a heavy habit. Three packs a day when I'm counting and honest; two packs a day when I'm not.

But finally I was confronted with the word—"you should not"—and then with my choice—"I will not."

I was and am still sometimes cold with fright.

Who, me? Without a cigarette?

Learning not to smoke is for people with guts, not for me.

11

Why tackle a pre-destined failure?

I do not have the strength it must take to put cigarettes out of my life, my mind cried out to me. But my heart said, "Try. Make a choice." It was through tears, lots of them, that I decided I'd find out—is this a thing that finally I can't do? Finally? Even for fifteen minutes?

Everybody who loves me wished that I could, but wouldn't bet a cent on it.

Maybe it was their lack of faith?

Maybe it was their derision?

Maybe it was good sense, finally poking through the smoke screen which surrounded me?

Whatever it was and is, I grew and grow determination.

I had and have some helps, some aids, some ways to help get me unhooked from nicotine. Are there any ways, short of commitment to an asylum? short of a straight jacket? short of one of those aversion therapy clinics you can't buy in theory or afford in money?

Are there any every-day ways to help you get unhooked even while you continue to be in the place you are?

Of course there are.

There are twenty-five ways which I write about now, and there will be more that you may want to write about as you discover them. There are places in this book, usually at chapters' ends, where you may become involved in written reaction to what you've read, to express what you are feeling about the commonality of all addictions (like ours to nicotine) and about the conquest of that addiction. People who cannot control the way they use or abuse food, alcohol, drugs, anger, tears have said that they found help with the aids in this book.

Personal power—you-power—is the nemesis of any addiction.

Conquest can be yours because you have the power to choose WINNING.

You are powerful enough to make a choice.

You will find emphasis in this book on the possibility of choice.

Not once in this book will you find a sermon exhorting you to "quit" smoking or "stop" smoking. You have either made that choice before this book came into your hands, or you are thinking about freeing yourself from nicotine. The motivation is yours, the motivation to do a positive thing—to learn how to live without cigarettes.

A teen-ager told me she could not quit—"I've been on 'em too long, for four years, since I was 12." A 30-year-old insurance man said, "Quit! I've tried! It's impossible! I've been smoking for ten years!"

I didn't suggest to them that they quit.

I suggested that they learn something new, learn how to go through a day without the crutches they were buying 20 to a pack.

Giving smokers something to do, rather than to un-do, was a heavy but positive assignment. Learning came to mean studying many life situations without the insidious gratification of a cigarette. Because they had motivation and some positive pick-ups to use during the difficult times, they learned a new skill—living without cigarettes.

Stop isn't my word. It's theirs. The teenager said, "I had to read all the time, over and over, what you wrote about stopping smoking. I called it my own stop-smoking book." The insurance man said, "What you wrote about stopping smoking got me through to my biggest accomplishment—stopping smoking."

They were dumbfounded when they found that nowhere in the carbon-smudged pages were the words "stop smoking."

"But that's what it's all about," he said.

"Even if you don't say so in those two words," she said.

It comes out to this, we decided:

Do I choose to use nicotine?

Do I choose to use my strength?

How do I hold the fort while I find my strength?

With the 25 fort-holders that follow, plus others you will discover, that is how.

You will develop your own crisis-fighters, your own personal intervention-ers.

Until you do, borrow mine.

They are tangible, useable, real.

Maybe only 10 of them will mean anything to you.

Maybe only one.

If one works, who needs 10 or 20?

I did and do, but then I am addicted to nicotine.

Worse than you.

The Important Because

My choice was not out of fear.

I made a choice out of love.

Choosing not to smoke is an act of love—love of the people who love you, and most certainly, the very legitimate love of yourself.

My husband, Mac, asked "Could you try . . . .?"

My oldest daughter, Toni, my strongest, most determined, obstinate, wonderful daughter said she wasn't coming home any more if I smoked. She's strong enough to mean it.

My younger, softer, quieter daughter, Molly, said with tears in her eyes, "Mom, it means so much to me for you not to smoke." She unglued me.

My older sons, Mike and Pat and Paul, said, "You're smelling up the house, the car, the everything."

My younger sons, Jamie and Kevin asked, "Don't you want to see us grow up?" Everybody's kids ask that.

My kids, your kids, my neighbor kids, your neighbor kids, your little brothers and sisters, your grandchildren, so many kids have us nailed to the wall with that line. They're brainwashed at school and come home to beseech us.

If you're choosing to be free, why? How come you've reached the decision that you are better than cigarettes are, that you're more important than your addiction?

What's your motive in making this choice to change the very way you breathe? It is as radical and momentous as that—changing the way you breathe. Why are you going to do it?

People who don't smoke because their doctors said "don't smoke" are the rare ones. If they can not smoke because somebody else said quit then they are different from me, and I think from you.

Didn't six doctors tell me to quit? Didn't I succeed in ignoring their advice and dwelling on the fact that three of them are still smoking? Or were they all more influential than I know?

Consciously, I made my choice not out of fear (if fear worked, every tobacco plantation in the world would have been replanted in soybeans or something else as innocuous in the dozen years since the Surgeon General's report.)

One of my friends chose not to smoke because he found he couldn't play his flute and saxophone as well as he used to. Poor lung-breath power. Poor circulation in his fingers. His motive in choosing not to smoke is that cigarettes were making something less of what he loved. Another friend likes to play a great game of tennis, only lately it wasn't so great. He knew smoking was wrecking his wind and his game. He chose not to smoke, to win in several ways, he said.

Survival, saxaphone, tears, tennis, kids—whatever, whoever, the reason has got to be YOUR reason. Others can give you reasons. Only you can take one.

It is rarely possible for a veteran smoker to choose on a whim not to smoke.

There must be strong motivation.

Strong motivation these days can be the hard fact that you're annoying so many people when you smoke in their presence. It could be that you're getting damn weary of shoveling smoke against the tide of disapproval.

Maybe you're choosing not to smoke because you want to shake off the addicting force which rules you.

It is good to sit with hands quiet and composed, or with arms resting comfortably around somebody, without the mad pawing for cigarettes, fire, ashtray. It is good not to have to muster the crusty indifference it takes nowadays to mess up everybody else's air.

There is a joy in the quietness of your hands; there is eventually a relief in seeing fingers which aren't clutching at a burning stick of impoliteness, pollution, the symbol of an insidious power over you.

In order to reach these peaks—the liberation, the quietness—define your motive, or motives, for choosing not to smoke. Find good ones, strong ones. Write them down in this book. Remember these motives. Write them down whenever you have a few minutes to kill, during the minutes you used to use for lighting up.

Your motives are yours.

So they're worth something.

So are you.

● ● ●

People told me about their motives; I'll list some of them. Write about yours and about others you learn about from your friends.

A middle-aged man (about 60)—"I want to choose to stop before a doctor tells me I must."

A teen-age boy (nearly 20)—"My parents said they'd pay for a week's ski trip every year for the next five years if I'd give them my word I wouldn't smoke for five years."

A woman in her prime (about 40)—"My family says my smoking makes them miserable."

17

The Ways

These are some of the WAYS
to help you get unhooked
from nicotine.
Each WAY is a tangible to touch when life without cigarettes
seems intolerable.

They are:
time-stoppers
crisis-smashers
fort-holders
wait-it-outers
tiny armistices.

Find the WAYS and the words, and make them yours, to
remind you that
You are bigger than nicotine
You are more powerful than your addiction.

These are WAYS to try when you're so scared that you think
you can never make it, never get unhooked. They are the
WAYS which worked for me and for friends as severely
addicted as I am.
I say "am" because I am.
Addicted.
Just for right now, I am choosing not to use.

Way 1
Enjoy Smoke

Psyche yourself into liking other people's smoke.

Face that smoke and tell yourself you love it.

Face this hard fact—lots of people you love are smokers.

You do not have to deny yourself their love and friendship just because you choose now not to smoke, and they are still using.

Instead, seek them out and tell them what a favor they are doing for you by smoking near you, very near you.

Otherwise, they may avoid you just like you avoided ol' Pete and Susie when you heard they were trying to get unhooked.

You can handle choosing not to smoke. I know you can, because I did.

What I could not handle, what you cannot handle, is the loss of people. So tell yourself that people who smoke are your allies. They are helping you. Their smoke is your smoke.

Watching somebody else light up is a plus for you. Convince yourself of that. Tell your head you want to be near somebody's smoke, but you do not want it pouring in and out of you. The worst room for me as I first began to come unhooked from nicotine was the room in which there was no smoke at all. I sought out pipe smokers and cigar smokers especially, because their lovely clouds and aroma enveloped me and their smoke was and is still like a salve to my raw nerves when I want a cigarette.

Smokers like us (who need these words, this book and the words and WAYS you are discovering) are usually fascinating people.

The people addicted to nicotine, as I am and you are, are almost always lovable, pat-able, huggable because we share a need for crutches—20 to a pack. It's hard to warm to a stone god or a vice-free goddess who needs no crutches.

It's difficult to empathize with people who don't want empathy.

We do, and we found some of it for years in the warmth of a cigarette in our hands, its small heat generating a glowing confidence in ourselves, a closeness to other smokers. At least, we thought that's what we had. What we had, in fact, was a hiding place.

As you come out from that hiding place, from behind that smoke cover, don't be hesitant to use others' covers for yours.

Enjoy second-hand what you don't want first-hand.

Tell yourself that it's wonderful to be near people who are lighting up constantly.

Empty their ashtrays.

Do not disdain them.

Instead, lean closer and smell their smoke. Let your family and friends know that their cigarettes are helpful to you, and learn to believe it.

What you can't bear is people avoiding you.

What you can bear, what you want, the sooner the better, are the marvelous consequences of your choice, "I CHOOSE not to smoke . . ."

Way 2
Watch Your Language

It's important never to say "I quit." Quit, quitter, quitting, are ugly words, that only remind you of those unctious, grinning, righteous brothers and sisters who ran around a few years ago wearing those "I quit" buttons.

Made me want to vomit, right after I snarled at the pious person and smashed the button to bits.

You are not quitting, you are CHOOSING not to smoke. You will announce that fact often and loud and wherever and whenever. Despite the fact that you are hooked (anybody reading and needing this book is hooked, as I am) you are making a choice. Remind everybody that it is your choice.

It is not your doctor, or the American Cancer Society, or your children, or your spouse, or your lover who's forced you to "give up smoking." You are not doing anything as grim as "giving it up"—like a sacrifice, like a penance.

You are choosing not to smoke because not to smoke is what you want for you. You have made the decision. It is of your own doing. It is your responsibility. You will grow into that responsibility.

You will ACHIEVE your own LIBERATION.

You will make a CONQUEST personally.

You're choosing (*you*, with the nicotine-stained fingers) to be responsible for your own unhooking. And you're going to talk about your liberation, and how it comes about. And about the pain of withdrawal. And about the joy in living up to your choice.

You will have lots to hang on to as you prolong your choice.

You will have faith in you, you will have the words you will write in this book, you will have the featured words—ACHIEVEMENT, LIBERATION, CONQUEST, and ACCOMPLISHMENT—to move toward.

We who truly are addicted to nicotine are usually people high on ACCOMPLISHMENT, super-motivated toward finding it. We're the kind who push hard for accomplishment, and because we push we've come to allow ourselves the extras—the third pack of cigarettes a day, just one more drink, maybe a pill or four? Now that we've decided to battle one of the extra pushers—nicotine—is the time to bring to bear all the same forces that bring accomplishment in other endeavors.

Think hard on a time when you were sure "I could never do that—" whatever "that" was.

Was it to land a big contract, to make a baked Alaska, to paint a seascape, to kick your indolent teenager out of the house, to move away from your dream house? But you *did*. You have done things so much harder and rougher than learning not to smoke. Count those things up, the things you dreaded, the things you feared, and dwell on success.

Don't look back on failure. Forget the other times you thought you'd get unhooked from nicotine. You did not then have the motivation you've got now.

Now you *know* you don't want to smoke anymore.

You want to be free from cigarettes.

You want the personal, *liberating* ACHIEVEMENT that can be yours.

Maybe you think you and ACHIEVEMENT are strangers.

Everybody has times in their life when they feel like they've only chased ACHIEVEMENT and never caught it. Here's a chance for a sure catch.

Take credit right now for achievement.

You're reading, you're contemplating making a choice against nicotine and for achievement, and you haven't smoked a cigarette since you started reading? Or you are delaying lighting one right now? Announce that fact to yourself, to anybody near by. Maybe you've begun to achieve and just need to know it.

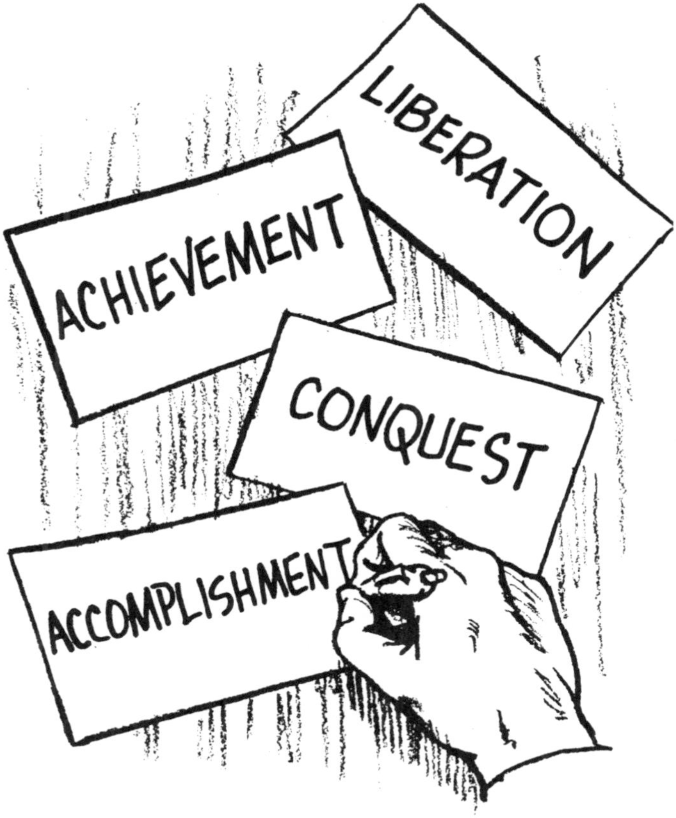
LIBERATION
ACHIEVEMENT
CONQUEST
ACCOMPLISHMENT

Every ten minutes can be a test, a mark of LIBERATION. Every small crisis that you meet cold—without a cigarette—can be a small unlinking. So can every moment of depression. There will be some depression. It's one of the prices you'll pay for liberation. Use the crises, the depression, the wanting, to see how it can be. Use them as measuring sticks of what you can take. You have the courage to do it. I know, because I don't know anyone as weak as I am, and I am doing it. You will, too, because it's so great to say, "I choose to get unhooked, to be liberated."

The first whole day of your CONQUEST—your win over your wanting—will be memorable. The first day you live without a cigarette may leave you looking outwardly whipped, but inside you'll have this fantastic sense of standing TALL because you are bigger than your addiction.

Write it out, on this page, in big and joyous letters, the seven-word capital contract with yourself. I CHOOSE TO BE FREE FROM CIGARETTES.

Get some marking pens in lots of different colors.

Write, print, doodle with the words ACCOMPLISHMENT, ACHIEVEMENT, LIBERATION, CONQUEST, JOY, CREDIT, FREEDOM, UN-HOOKING, in lines and spaces below your contract. Print your name, sign your name, scribble your name, in arrays of colors and sizes. Write your name on top of ACCOMPLISHMENT and accomplishment will be yours.

Write their names—those words, ACCOMPLISHMENT, ACHIEVEMENT, CONQUEST, LIBERATION—on small papers to put in your pockets, your purse, your desk, your cupboards, your tackle-box, your cosmetic case, your golf bags, in the places where you live. You will come across them when you need them.

Print the words poster-size to hang up as temporary wall-coverings. When friends ask, "How come you tacked up that big piece of paper that says ACCOMPLISHMENT in your living room?" tell them it's a map of where you're going.

Way 3
Light Fires

Light a lot of matches, incense, candles, fireplace fires, bonfires, any kind of fires. Use matches, lots of matches. Use your cigarette lighter. Click it, watch it spark, look at the flame, lots of times. Smell something burning.

Use the accoutrements of smoking. Set fire to incense in an ashtray. Your biggest and best ashtray holds three candles. Set them in there and light the candles. Your favorite ashtray can be a candle-holder. Set one candle in it, light it, look at the lovely smoke, blow it out to make more smoke, light it again.

See ashtrays, fire and smoke, cigarette holders, cigarette bags.

Don't deny yourself the look of some of your favorite things.

The fire and smoke can be near you even if the fire isn't on the end of a cigarette and the smoke coming out of your mouth.

Keep near you the old, familiar, dear things.

Hang on to the same sounds.

Some of a cigarette's grip on those of us who are hooked is the action of the match striking, the sound of the lighter clicking, the look of smoke, the sight of fire. So burn something. Make smoke.

There are places, of course, where that'll be a no-no. Where you won't be able to get a bunch of candles going, or fire up on incense.

Your friends and family are expecting you to be a little strange these days, but strangers may not understand your strangeness if you should carry a lighted candle into the bus depot.

But in places where you can—the dear, familiar places—use the little warmth of a candle, use the scent of incense, to somewhat fill up the tobaccoless void you are in.

Explain to people who care, or to those who merely stare, what you are doing. Today you will find more acceptance to your small insanities than you will to your cigarette smoke. It's acceptable to be somewhat demented while you are getting unhooked from nicotine. People will allow you lots of idiosyncracies during withdrawal. Fill your apartment or home with the thick smell or incense, of wax, or whatever, all scents that can be inhaled.

Burn the incense and wax in those familiar things, things you'd miss if they weren't around. You can have them, use them, without cigarettes. That favorite ashtray can be right where it's always been. It is not like the coffin holding the deceased. It means new life to you. It is, empty of ashes and butts, an intimate friend which will give some semblance of sameness to your days.

Your days won't be the same, when you decide "I choose to be free from cigarettes." They'll be better. So very much better. Eventually.

Way 4
Run from the Righteous

You don't need right now to hear from anybody who says, "I just laid cigarettes down and never thought about them again" or who asks, "How could you possibly want one of those dirty things?"

People who talk like that are insensitive clods who don't understand what nicotine means to us, what it means to be hooked.

They don't know how much of our lives is wound up in the love-hate relationship we have with cigarettes.

I love cigarettes and hate them for the grip they have on me. I love cigarettes so much that except for the times I was actively engaged in showering, sex, childbirth, sleep or under anesthesia, I had a cigarette going.

So the person who tells me, "I just decided one day not to smoke and it didn't bother me at all" makes me feel like a spineless, gutless, worthless chimney, full of the cold ashes of self-dislike.

The person who cannot understand your misery right now doesn't deserve you. You need a happy unhooked person, somebody who knows your current kind of hell, who was there, who can make you laugh (grin, at least?) over the stories of their suffering.

Talking, weeping, laughing with the non-righteous helps to make it bearable. The saintly ones who never suffered when they "just laid 'em down and forgot 'em" are not our kind of people. Let them go talk to each other.

You deserve better.

Find that person. The search may take you beyond your neighborhood, your co-workers, your bridge club, the Elks Lodge, etc. Strike up conversations, instead of matches, with people who have interesting, sensitive faces. Ask them, "Did you ever smoke?" And "if you did and aren't now, how come? How did you do it?" Let them know, if you feel safe with them, that you need some help. Give them importance in your choosing not to smoke, as you choose each other for friends.

Write down the things they said that you want to remember. One of the women I talked to was humming a happy song as she emptied ashtrays in her beauty salon. I asked Natalie if she had helped fill them and she said no, that she'd learned how not to smoke and was glad she did but she wasn't the least bit pompous about it. So I brightened to her and asked if she had a favorable crisis-stopper when she was first getting unhooked. She said when the desire for nicotine really waved over her, she would say to herself, "But I just put one out" and try to find that feeling of just having butted one out. It helped her. You can learn from others their conspiracies with themselves, if they are a sharing, caring kind of person, like you are.

Write them down. List the ways other people have convinced themselves they could choose not to smoke. List some telephone numbers for your own private hotline. Call the real Hotline or the agency in your area that has sympathetic ears. Talk about cigarettes. Talk about your choice to be a user no longer. Do it NOW.

My own personal hotline-helping names and numbers:

_____

_____

_____

_____

_____

_____

_____

_____

As you make known to others your choice for freedom from cigarettes, you will learn why and how other people made the choice. Sometimes the stories are interesting enough to jot down. Some examples are:

Betty: She wanted "to buy some time at the other end."

Ruth: She had to tell her daughter, Francie, that she'd have to give up her cat because of her brother's allergy. Ruth felt it only fair that the day they left "Fuzzy" at his new home, would be the day she smoked her last cigarette. It was.

Ben: His wife said no more kisses or anything if he continued to smoke. He wanted kisses and everything.

Jerry: He blew smoke through a handkerchief, saw the yellow residue it left there and was revolted.

Evelyn: She was forced to stop—strep throat—couldn't swallow at all. "When I was healthy again, I decided it wasn't worth starting anew. And that was nine years ago."

Lila: She works in a health education office, and decided her smoking contradicted what she was trying to teach.

Cousin Babe: She, after smoking 20 years, decided that it was wasting her time. She held a pencil between two fingers where there had always been a cigarette, chewed on it a lot, and imagined, and amazed her family by her choice to be free.

Way 5
Don't Not Think About Cigarettes

You are going through real bereavement. Cigarettes have been close and dear and constant, like a member of the family, like a beloved friend. You cannot ignore losing them now any more than you could ignore grief.

Bereavement. It is long and hard and it hurts. It is helpful to me, in my hard choice to unhook from nicotine, to think long and hard on other people's current, really tragic bereavements. I think of my friend, Ann, whose husband, one sunny, perfect day for sailing, was drowned. I think of my cousin, Marcella, who had to watch her child die of leukemia. We each know people whose real grief is greater than the one we know now when we choose not to smoke.

When I think I simply cannot face the day without smoking, I ask myself, "How is Ann facing this day, and all her days, without Burt?" or "If Marcella could smile at that child lying there, knowing she had to plan her funeral, how dare I be so weak about a weed?"

But allow yourself a sense of loss, your very personal loss. You are bereft without cigarettes. Admit it to yourself, and tell others that you feel bereaved.

If it helps, cry a lot or a little. Tears are acceptable, usable, and they wash away so much. They are healthier for you, whoever you are, than setting up the smoke-screen you have been using to protect you.

You will feel psychologically naked for a while when you don't have a cigarette and its smoke to clothe and to cover the ways that you feel things.

Expect that you will feel defenseless.

Expect that you will feel as if your raw nerve ends are being trodden or twisted by almost everybody or anything you encounter.

Expect to hurt, to want.

And gear for it. With the right words, the right attitudes, the right people near by.

You can face anything if you know its look before it gets to you.

Live again in your memory the worst nightmare, waking or sleeping, you've ever had. Usually, once you know its look, you can face it. That's the way it is with some of the hard parts of learning to be free from nicotine. Do not run from the image of how bad you think it's going to be. Face that image.

YOU CAN FACE ANYTHING IF YOU KNOW ITS LOOK BEFORE IT GETS TO YOU.

Congratulate yourself inwardly, out-loudly, about each hour you are free, each conquest you make of a smoking situation.

Your courage shall have, is having, joy to match when you put down an unlit match, set down an unlit cigarette, and fight emotionally and psychologically to be free.

One day somebody's going to say to you, "My Gawd! I didn't think you could go a day without a cigarette. You're really something!"

Way 6
Earn While You Learn

Some people are allowed to smoke while they work.

Some people aren't. They have to gauge their whole being toward that next cigarette break. A lot of us think that work and smoke are synonymous. Who can live through a normal day on the job, let alone survive a traumatic day, without cigarettes?

I am a newspaper reporter and writer. It was impossible for me to begin a story without beginning a cigarette. It would be impossible to stay on top of a really rough interview without one cigarette or six. When the right words refuse to write, when the interview subject is cagey, there has to be the quick brightness that a match and nicotine bring for me to continue, for me to write, for me to have a job, for me to earn a living, for me to be me, for me to survive. Smoking and writing are as much of a steadfast pair in my life as are my twin sons. I couldn't have one without the other. To have only one would destroy me. Yet there was this day when I said, partly because of my love for those twin sons, that "I CHOOSE to be free . . ."

I could not say "my career be damned." For lots of reasons. Because I am not me unless I write. Because I need the stimulation and challenge of a job with a daily newspaper. Because we need my income (two sons in college, four children still living at home). So I had to learn to write without first lighting up, and it was a bitch.

I paced, I chewed gum, I ate sunflower seeds, I nearly sobbed out loud. I ran outside the building so I could holler at myself in the parking lot. I made nine starts with every story, each start lousier than the one before. I wrote some obituaries one morning and forgot to say who died.

When I tried to write at home, I burned a lot of incense and candles, and cherished every line that went on paper because, good or bad, it was at least a line of something. I'd send the stuff I'd written whilst not smoking to critical newspaper editors. They told me it didn't show! That my torment hadn't wrecked my work! That the stuff was passable, printable, even good! Unbelievable!

I sit back now and light a match. Because I'm having trouble writing these next lines. The match, the sulfur, the action, the warmth, the smoke, all do something for me. Enough so that I can hope to write these words well: regardless of what your job is, regardless of how many people around you smoke, regardless of the pressures, the politics, the pinch of the position, *you can work and not smoke.*

If I can, anybody can.

For years I'd said, "As soon as I finish this next writing project, I'll quit smoking." How wrong I was to figure I had to wait, how negative to use the word "quit."

I had to learn to choose to do a positive thing. The positive learning, instead of the negative "giving up." For me, the process began to work on the job. I thought I could never work unless my cigarette was lit, but I began to relate my resolve (to do a good job on the job) to my determination to be loyal to my choice (to live without nicotine).

Co-workers offer a mixed bag of helps and hurts. Those who smoke may outwardly and loudly congratulate you, while they hate your guts. Others who have learned not to smoke, or who have never smoked, might be laying odds that you'll never make it.

The thing I had to learn to do on my job was to be my own challenger. To be me against the clock. Me against the deadline. Me against the pressure. Me against me. Me in command. I felt lousy when I let me down and smoked. I felt

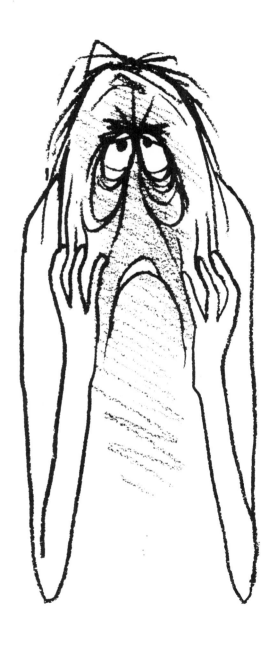

good about myself each time I respected me and my choice—to be free from cigarettes.

Eventually I learned that I worked faster, sharper, brighter after I had unlearned smoking. I said things better verbally and in print when my head (and the air) was clear.

I realized gradually how I had slowed myself down for years with the hesitations and interruptions I allowed myself every time I lit a cigarette.

You can't realize now the way it will be, not now when you'd like to roll the pages of this book into cigarettes and smoke 'em.

Maybe this will be a mind-popper.

Is there any job that is done better by a person smoking?

Is there any kind of work in the world that a man or woman does better while smoking? I can think of only two—posing for a cigarette commercial or being used as a human guinea pig in a lung lab.

Right now you may think that without tobacco as an ally you can't function in whatever your role is in life. Would you take it from somebody who learned bitterly that it's just not true?

You will be better at whatever you do, when you get unhooked.

You may even get a raise or a promotion. Not because you've put cigarettes down, but because you've put yourself up and have the confidence in yourself that tells the world, and management, "I am in command of me. I am somebody new."

Write about how it was today on the job, at the office, at school, how it was when your hands, mouth and lungs were empty of cigarettes, or how it was when you blew it.

_____

_____

_____

_____

Way 7
Therapy, for Fee or Free

Talking about our determination not to use nicotine.

That's therapy.

That's the tool that was my turning-point, the WAY that is way out in front in usefulness.

Schedule it. Plan when and where. That's important.

You didn't learn your profession, vocation or avocation by chance, did you? It took concentrated study and work to earn you your kind of success.

It will take concentrated study and work to unlearn your involvement with cigarettes. Don't leave the unlearning to chance. It's by choice you are learning to be free from nicotine.

So choose up all the aids you can find to help you keep your choice. One of the best aids is talking it over with someone who understands, maybe somebody who has fought a battle like yours and won. Some people are good to be with even though they've never known our kind of addiction. Maybe they've known and conquered other addictions—addictions to food, alcohol, drugs.

Set up a definite time every day, or every other day, when you can talk with this friend about smoking, about your choice to be free.

The paid friends—psychiatrists, psychologists, social workers—are good to have if they are not themselves addicted to nicotine. It is difficult to feel deep-down that a counselor can help if you know that counselor can hardly wait for you to leave before lighting up.

A friend-for-free who really can help is one who's battled nicotine, or drugs, or alcohol, or their mother-in-law, or the crabgrass and won.

The important thing is to find that person who wants you to win. Find that person who wants to share in your choice and your victory.

Talk it out, beginning with why you started to smoke.

If you started to smoke as one form of rebellion against your parents and you are now 45 years old, then your reason is gone.

Did you start to smoke because everybody in your senior high school crowd smoked? You haven't seen much of the ol' gang for 15 years? So where's the peer pressure?

You began to smoke because people said you could control your weight by smoking? Now you've got the weight of a heavy habit, plus the pounds? Do the scales say there's more of you?

Perhaps you learned to smoke because you thought it gave you a suave, sophisticated look? Because you thought a cloud of smoke swirling between your face and his, or hers, was seductive? Today, sophistication is the all-together look of somebody who doesn't need to be clutching at a burning pacifier.

Let go. Let go of the pack.

Leave your pack in another room, and walk back to your friend and say, "This is my choice, to let go and leave them some place else."

Then talk some more about the "whys" and the "how muches"—the "whys" of your getting hooked, the "how muches" of your need, such as how much you enjoy cigarettes when in actuality you can't remember how it used to be without them. Can you remember a YOU without them?

Memories make for laughing and crying, sometimes simultaneously, as you discover the lies you've been feeding yourself to justify your addiction, and as you discover the strength and resolve within you to choose to stop feeding that addiction.

You will be bewildered sometimes at what you learn about yourself.

Some things you never analyzed will surface. You'll remember the good times and the bad. You'll remember how cigarettes came to dominate so many scenes in your life. How maybe they cost you a position in the varsity team line-up? How maybe you finished fourth in the track event that used to be all yours? How you missed an important lecture and the "A" you needed because it seemed more important to leave to have a cigarette? How you wanted to break out of the receiving line at your own wedding reception to have a smoke? How a great moment in a stage play was lost for you because the urge to have a cigarette crowded out the other drama? How you once denied yourself the joy of holding a new baby because you were holding a cigarette? how you left someone's hospital bedside repeatedly to have a cigarette?

Now, think of yourself without a cigarette in your hand, of you without cigarettes in your shirt pocket, in your purse. Get used to the look, to the picture. With your friend near you, you won't panic.

If I can be that friend, with these words, let me be. But I hope for you that there's a real body near you, somebody sane and secure and smiling, sans cigarette. Like the Betty I had and have.

Maybe you'll light up as soon as you separate, as I did once or twice. I disliked myself a lot for that. Here somebody who cared had just spent three hours with me, and I could hardly wait for her to get in her car and drive away so I could smoke! My chagrin lasted the rest of the day and kept me nicotine-free.

You'll find yourself wondering as you butt out a bootlegged cigarette one day, "Was that my last one?"

I cannot celebrate the anniversary of my first whole day without a cigarette.

I did not think consciously one May morning as I butted one out that it was my last.

I was so sure I could not be strong enough to stay with my choice. Almost no one thought I could. A few said "You can and you will" and a few smiled at me and kept faith in me. Surely, there's somebody in your life like that, even if you have to borrow the body and the spirit from a member of the American Cancer Society chapter where you live.

We smokers usually are people who attract people. Our human-ness, our frailties, the same characteristics which support our need for cigarettes usually make us lovable. But fewer and fewer people like our fire.

We used to be the center of a smoking group. Now we're the butts of a society screaming at us, "You're messing up our air!" Somewhere, find that person who doesn't scream at you. Maybe it's a somebody not in your circle right now, maybe somebody you know casually but admire.

I called my friend-who-became-therapist and said, "How did you do it? You smiled as you did not smoke and you used to smoke like a furnace?" She came over to talk, to tell me.

The right person wants to help. Like my friend, who said, "Sure, I miss cigarettes, but I'm so happy I choose not to smoke, and I want to help you in the same choice. . . ." There is that person. Find that person. And use that person's understanding to help you to get unhooked.

I used the word "use" purposefully. You have a right, right now, to use people who sincerely want to help you. Lean on them as they may have leaned on somebody, and one day people will be leaning on you asking, "How did you do it? How come you're not smoking? Would you help me?"

I know. It's happening now to me. And it will to you.

Fantasize on that and know that it does not have to always be a fantasy.

Way 8
Be Another You

Patterns. I know you can't avoid waking up. But you can wake up to new ways. You can take a lot of showers, engage in much bicycling, prayer, sex, tennis, swimming. You can go to church.

You can hang around some places where smoking is not permitted. They're getting easier and easier to find.

Among the little ways I changed the way my days ordinarily ran was to not read the Los Angeles *Times'* editorial pages when I usually read them—at 6 a.m. with coffee and cigarettes, much coffee, many cigarettes.

When I chose to eliminate one important element—the cigarettes—of my morning triumvirate of pleasures, the impact of the loss sent me running out of the house and up the street. Jogging in your robe, with tears streaming down your face, is a lil' freaky even for my neighborhood. Some people saw me, some people heard me cursing "Goddamit, I sure need a cigarette" and then promising myself..."but right now I choose not to have one." On these mornings I was a ridiculous sight, but remember, we are allowed our small insanities while learning to live without nicotine.

If you drive a lot and smoke a lot while you drive, try to arrange with your business or the boss or the family that you not be confined to your car quite so much for the first few weeks of your new life-style. Cigarettes can be such great company when driving solo. They're rotten when mixed company—smokers and non-smokers—is trapped in the same car. Realizing how your smoke used to gag your non-smoking passengers can help you through a nicotine crisis.

If TV-watching is cigarette-time for you, watch less TV. Go see a movie at a theater which doesn't permit smoking (do any of them anymore?) and hold your head high, smile valiantly when other people light up as soon as they leave the theater. They need a weed. You don't.

If you really want to astound yourself with the number of times you rely on nicotine, check off the times you light up, or used to:

_____ whenever you woke up
_____ with the first cup of coffee
_____ with the second cup of coffee
_____ with all cups of coffee
_____ as you shaved
_____ as you put on your make-up
_____ as you drove to work or market
_____ while you shopped
_____ before every phone call
_____ to accompany all decision-making
_____ during every trip to the bathroom
_____ when you felt an argument brewing
_____ during an argument
_____ when you lost the argument
_____ when you won
_____ with every drink
_____ after every snack or meal
_____ before sex
_____ after sex
_____ just before you slept

Each of these situations may have happened three times a day, or each happening may have taken three cigarettes. Whatever. It adds up to a lot of cigarettes, but I know the panic of having only the drink, not the cigarette. Dissolve the panic this way. Concentrate on the drink as you never did before. Hold the glass with both hands. Endow that drink with the kicks you get, or used to get, from both alcohol and nicotine.

If you feel you are addicted to both unhook one addiction at a time. Conquering one will give you strength to tackle the other. I know veteran members of Alcoholics Anonymous who have finally now learned not to lean on nicotine.

My roughest hurdle was going to be trying to enjoy a cup of coffee without a cigarette, I thought. I feared that so!

Then I found it was not intolerable!

I had psyched myself into believing that the coffee could give me everything I needed just then. I put a pencil where a cigarette used to be. Sometimes I used the pencil to write in a little book, or on the back of an envelope. I wrote anything to keep my hands and head busy. I wrote and write words now about how marvelous I was and am for gripping only the coffee cup and the pencil, and not a nicotine stick.

Invest the coffee-drinking with the same joy you used to think you got from nicotine and coffee. Coffee alone can be a comfort.

So can any new surprising way you create to live your day. Take time to think of, to plan, variations on your old theme of a cigarette-to-go-with-everything.

You go, with all your systems turned to "on" and liberation.

Right now your hobby is smoking. Call it a hobby, a habit, a vice. Whatever it is, you can't think of anything you'd trade it for.

I submit you'd like to trade it for the accomplishment, the achievement, the exhilaration, the joy of saying "I choose not to smoke", and your pride in being loyal to your choice.

I tried to think of something that would make up to me for my loss, of something to comfort me in my bereavement. I thought of adultery. If smoking is a vice, I'd give up one for the other. But adultery is awkward in a lot of situations and places where I used to have a cigarette—the office, a restaurant, the supermarket.

So I took up plant raising. Plants didn't interest me or excite me at first. There were times when I'd pinch the buds right off an azalea because of my anger over not having a cigarette. But there were other times when I'd grab the earth or some potting mix and revel in the fact that my hands were full of something that was not burning me down.

A friend took up photo-processing and locked himself away in a place where he could not smoke. It diverted him for some of the time.

Another friend took up jogging and macrame. She said she couldn't do either while she smoked.

Photography, jogging, macrame—none is the total answer to what you do with the frustrations and tensions that build when you choose not to smoke.

But they are something to do for some of the time.

If you have enough of these crisis-interventionists, there will be hours that pass when it is EASIER not to have a cigarette.

And that's what you're trying to do. You're trying to make it EASIER to live without cigarettes until you reach the point where it would be HARD to have a cigarette.

There is that place and that point.

Until you reach it, find distracting, diverting, imaginative things to do, and maybe distracting, diverting, imaginative people to do them with.

Find an avocation different from your usual ones. If you crochet, and smoke, don't figure that taking up crewel is going to be a switch. Take up swimming.

If you are naturally involved in athletic things, find another past-time totally unrelated to a physical thing. Try studying a new religion.

If you are a collector—stamps, coins, butterflies, recipes—and spend a lot of time at that hobby, get one that takes you away from the collection, and from your collection of ash trays.

Get into a slim-and-trim class. You can't light up while you're doing push-ups.

Divert your mind and hands to other entanglements while you untangle the octopi-hold nicotine has on you. Fantasize how each new diversion unsticks one of tobacco's tentacles from you. It's good dreaming! Better than that, it's a great happening and it's happening now.

Way 9
On Fantasies and Farewells

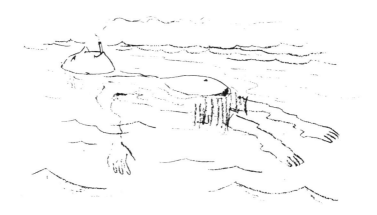

In this dramatic scene, you are the star.

Imagine with all of your being how it would be to take a cigarette from a pack, to place it between your lips, to fondle it with your lips and hands, to find a match or reach for your lighter, to light the thing, to inhale, and like WOW!

Utter ecstasy? Right?

Almost right?

Some doubt about it?

Any doubt about it?

Or have you realized yet that reality cannot possibly match your fantasy?

Nothing in this world smokes as good as your fantasy.

Nothing grows for real that is as fantastic to smoke as the cigarette your mind grows in your fantasy.

Remember when you blew it, a few hours ago or the other day, and smoked?

Was it really as great as you imagined it would be?

Or was it a disappointment?

The cigarettes I bootlegged (or you may be bootlegging, while choosing not to smoke) were and are disappointments to me. They didn't and don't match my dreams.

More painfully, I am a disappointment to me.

I learned through bitter disappointment in me, that nothing I could smoke came anywhere near providing the ecstasy with which I falsely endowed inhaling and exhaling smoke.

For 30 years I gave glories not rightfully theirs to cigarettes.

A cigarette would see me through any situation, crisis, boredom, challenge, anxiety. When a bunch of cigarettes didn't, I gave them another chance, and another, until I was lighting them when I didn't even know I was lighting them, when I really didn't want one, when they tasted rotten, when people I love turned away from me, because I was smoking, about to smoke or stunk of smoke.

Still I wasn't deterred.

My mother, old and ill with asthmatic bronchitis and heart disease, said, "Don't kiss me goodbye, you smell so bad of cigarettes." So I gave up kissing my mother.

Now, I can't tell her that if I had a chance to kiss her goodbye, I'd smell of good cologne and cinnamon chewing gum.

Kissing her goodbye has to be fantasy now.

It could have been for real.

I kept running away from my father's bedside during his last hours on earth so that I could go and have a cigarette. He was dying of lung cancer. For three years after his death, I smoked heavily, without hope. I had this self-defeating hoplessness that I had no choice, that I could not let cigarettes go.

That ugly hopelessness really had a hold on me. It has its hold on you. Throw it out.

Were there sad times in your life made more sad because of your ever-present cigarette? Cigarettes have been more than a nuisance, a habit, an oral pacifier, a hand-busier, a smoke-screen. They've been at times hurtful to people we love or loved. We sold ourselves fantasies to say they weren't.

We lived on fantasies—"I could stop smoking any time I want" and "Smoking isn't as dangerous as driving on the freeway" and "Smoking isn't hurting anybody but me, so I'll smoke if I want".

Now we know what's real. We know that stopping smoking is not done by whim; we know that smoking is more dangerous health-wise than driving, and we've learned that the air belongs to everyone and that non-smokers are getting uptight and downright protective about their air. We've had to give up those fantasies.

Now we've lived through another fantasy—the fantasy smoke—and the fantasy has forced us to realize what's real—cigarettes don't match our dream of them.

But you can match the dream of being the kind of person you want to be. That's the kind who can find personal power to make a choice for ACCOMPLISHMENT, ACHIEVEMENT, CON-QUEST, LIBERATION, to get unhooked.

There were times in your life when your cigarette and its smoke hurt somebody you loved, or love. Write some words about those times and about how differently the scene might play today.

_____

_____

_____

_____

Way 10

Non-Nicotine Num-Nums

Cigarettes seem to provide a kick, a kind of pizazz that says to you, "I can really get going on this project now that I've got a cigarette going."

It becomes clear, clearer, clearest, later, that cigarettes in themselves don't give you any extra drive. You are giving them a property that is yours. You gave or are giving to them a power that belongs to you. Because you gave away the drive, the impetus, the get-up-and-go, it went. To cigarettes.

How many times have you said or thought, "As soon as I have a cigarette, I can get started..." or "Just give me time for a cigarette, and then I can tackle that..." For years, you could have done it all sooner, without hesitation, without the waiting, without the props. But by this time you don't know that. You're so accustomed to hobbling with a nicotine crutch, that you have no confidence in you without that crutch.

So there will be this "I can't get started without a cigarette" feeling. There will be this depression, this black, unlit depression that gets blacker and blacker because you think, "I'm just no good until I light up."

Plan on its happening, and it won't be so bad when it does.

Line up ammunition against the let-down.

Find ammunition that will be your power-house, or can be endowed with energy-giving properties.

I stocked my desk, pockets, purse, car and kitchen, and bedroom with snacks from health food stores, and with bottles of high-protein capsules.

I don't know if they did me any good at all. I'm not a health-food addict, remember? I'm addicted to nicotine, but the strange foods I bought and stashed here and there did give me something to do with my hands and face and lips when I was not lighting up.

It was a new experience for me. Maybe it will be for you, too, to search out stuff in a health food store or at the food faddist section of the supermarket. I had never frequented those places. All I needed was cigarettes and coffee, remember?

But when you and I choose not to smoke, we'll grab whatever is available to put into our empty hands.

They have some pretty weird stuff in those natural food stores. Some of it is so strange that while you're studying the wrapper or eating the stuff you can almost forget you'd rather have a cigarette.

There are these mysterious tastes, these exotic consistencies of glucose with coconut, dextrose with carob, sunflower seeds with sauerkraut flavoring, blended kelp, parsley squares. How about some whipped soybean ragout?

Really turns you off, hey?

Go get some, anyway. The shopping can be preoccupying and besides, walking up and down the health food aisles can give you a virtuous glow that overwhelms the one on the tip of a cigarette.

Chomp on sesame seed squares.

Salami.

Cinnamon gum.

Spiced things seem to season down, to make less of that craving for nicotine. A case of fighting fire with fire? Chili peppers? Why not? If they're so hot they make you cry, good. Squeeze out a few tears in requiem for cigarettes.

Some of the new, strange foods you can find to munch on are so awful to eat you can swear and eat at the same time. Profanity and spice seem to go well together, while you're making your choice not to smoke. Want to find some way-out foods today and add them to the list here? How about underlining in red the ones that are best at helping you forget you want a cigarette? C'mon, there are at least two, maybe 12?

APPLES	PEPPERMINTS	RAH!! FOR RAW....
BOLOGNA	PECANS	COCOANUT
COFFEE	MARINATED MUSHROOMS	TURNIPS
CINNAMON GUM	PRUNES	CAULIFLOWER
SUNFLOWER SEEDS	SALAMI	PINEAPPLE
ANCHOVIES	RED HOTS (CANDIES)	RADISHES
PEPPERONI	SESAME SEEDS	CABBAGE
GUM BALLS	SALTED PEANUTS	GREEN PEPPER
CHUTNEY	BEEF JERKY	CARROTS
GORP (GOOD OL' RAISINS AND PEANUTS)	LICORICE	CELERY
	SHARP CHEESE	ZUCCHINI
TEA	SPICED PEACHES	CUCUMBER
TANGERINES	PICKLES	GRAPES
PIZZA	GRANOLA	ORANGES
CRACKERS	ARTICHOKES	PARSLEY
CROUTONS		CHERRIES
SPICY POTATO CHIPS		TOMATOES

Way 11

Congratulate You

There'll be days when the awareness of the way you want a cigarette is with you maddeningly the whole day.

Then there'll be tolerable days, when all your support systems are working, when you meet up with people who congratulate you sincerely, when your courage, verve and zest are all turned to high and goodbye nicotine.

Then there'll be days when you'll see yourself as the most piteous creature, when there's nothing inside you to say "I'm winning," when a plastic friend says "You'll never make it. I tried once and couldn't do it. Here, have one of mine."

Recognize right now that some users are hoping you won't make it.

They may tell you how marvelous you are, how much they admire you, and how they wished they had your determination.

Secretly, they're hoping you don't make it.

I know people act like this, because I did.

Years before I tried to unhook from nicotine, I'd rattle off compliments to somebody in the process of learning not to smoke, but inside me I'd be thinking, "If she makes it, then she's better than me because I can't live without them." I could hardly camouflage my delight when I saw her smoking again.

Write about the way you delighted yourself today when you managed hour after hour to not light up. Print CONGRATULATIONS in big letters if you were loyal to your choice today. Or write of your new determination for tomorrow if today was just too, too intolerable.

C O N G R A T U L A T I O N S TO ME! ! ! ! _____

Save the congratulations. I blew it today... _____

    I REALLY WANT A CIGARETTE
        BUT
                I DON'T HAVE TO HAVE ONE JUST BECAUSE I
WANT ONE

There are lots of things I want that I don't have.
I don't have:

a ski chalet at Gstaad .... yes ___ no ___
$500,000 in my checking account ..... yes ___ no ___
$5 in my checking account .... yes ___ no ___
a checking account .... yes ___ no ___
entre at the White House .... yes ___ no ___
a part in Paul Newman's new movie ... yes ___ no ___
a part in Goldie Hawn's new movie .... yes ___ no ___
a cigarette .... yes ___ no ___

I not only survive without any or many of the above, I can be happy without any of the above:

yes _____   no _____   sometimes _____

These are things I have:

a book .... yes ___ no ___
a pencil or pen .... yes ___ no ___
some time to use both .... yes ___ no ___
the good sense to use both—this book
    and this pen or pencil—like now ..... yes ___ no ___
control of what I do .... yes ___ no ___
a choice .... yes ___ no ___
the determination to keep my choice ... yes ___ no ___
one person to support me .... yes ___ no ___
_____ yes ___ no ___
_____ yes ___ no ___

Learning to be free from cigarettes is:

_____ a hard slow process
_____ getting me some compliments
_____ affecting my work
_____ getting easier
_____ giving me a rotten disposition
_____ making me cry
_____ one of my biggest accomplishments
_____ maddening
_____ a mean, dirty battle
_____ an achievement I'll always be proud of

Way 12
Ask God

How are you at praying? Done much? Done any?

Have you never quit praying? Or did you never learn?

It works really great for some people. For others, saying prayers seems like talking into a dead phone. Or maybe getting "no" for an answer?

I can't remember when I didn't pray. I remember getting "no" for an answer as often or oftener than "yes," but I still believe.

But it seemed damned ridiculous to pray silently or out loud, "God, I can't hack this. I can't go another 10 minutes without lighting a cigarette. Do you care, God?"

Maybe it's while you're waiting for an answer, maybe it's because there is a flood of reassurance that goes through you, that you find yourself grinning at the spectacle of you asking God to worry about your *almost* over-powering desire for a slim little satanic Svengali.

Or maybe you remember the other times you prayed—there must have been three or four times in your life when you were frightened enough to pray—and the memory of that time or those times will bring some tears, tears that scald, that reduce you yet awaken you to recognition that you need a bigger Somebody.

You are bigger in that recognition and would make Him a good partner because by this time in your thinking, you have, together, Him and you, become more of a match for those things you used to light with a match.

So light a match, light a flame, fire up a small votive candle whose wavering light could be a constant prayer, choose to say you will not fire up a cigarette.

Choose to say there isn't a God to help you, or choose to say there is one and that He or She is not too busy to remember that you need some help. So does the whole world. But right now, wherever you are you need some, too. Plus some kindness, some understanding, some loving. Sometimes there's not a human being around to give a damn. Sometimes there's not a warm body next to yours, or a hand that wants to hold yours. The dog's snarling and the cat's in hiding. In those times learning to live without cigarettes can be a solitary way to go.

But praying can combat successfully the craving.

Listen to me, I was there, I am there. Finally I told Him that nicotine seemed bigger than me and wasn't He going to help me?

Inside me there was an answer that said, "Well, a weed is certainly not bigger than God and there is no habit as enduring as God."

If at first prayer is uncomfortable, remember how unpracticed you are at asking help for yourself, and how skilled you are at lighting cigarettes. Learn to be as skilled in small, silent prayers.

Some seem unable to acknowledge God.

Try borrowing from Alcoholics Anonymous the idea of a Higher Power, a Supreme Being, a Somebody-bigger-than-you. If you can, use that idea of a figure beyond yourself in another realm Who cares about you.

If all that is alien to you, if you are uncomfortable with it, remind yourself that, God or no God, Him or Her, prayer or no prayer, you have the strength you choose to be free, and to keep the choice.

If you allow yourself prayers, scribble one out on this page. If not a prayer, write a new pledge to yourself, or renew that contract you made with yourself:

My prayer or pledge:

_____
_____
_____
_____
_____
_____
_____
_____
_____
_____

I choose to be free from cigarettes. _____
_____

Cigarettes will not control me. I will control me. _____
_____
_____
_____
_____
_____
_____

Way 13

Hang on to a Rock

Hold on tight to something with the same hand, the same fingers that used to hold a cigarette.

It could be one of those phoney cigarettes that look so real. At a crisis time, you could hang it from your mouth for some of the satisfaction the feel of a cigarette gives. It could be a pencil or pen, jammed between your lips when the need's acute. A candy cigarette? Maybe there's some reward in eating it. Forget the calories. A crisis-stopper sometimes is fattening. We need some toys, some sweetness to distract our thoughts from nicotine, to fill the empty hand and lips.

I used a rock to hold tight in my hands. Not a "pet rock," although I did pet mine a lot. My rock, small, smooth, was given to me by my six-year-old friend, Mia, who said it was her very favoritest thing in the whole world. I hung on to it. I cried on it. I think sometimes I bled on it.

It became, because of the power I gave it, a small replacement for inhaling and exhaling. I would, and I do, still hold that rock tight in my hand while I take deep, deep long breaths, inhaling and exhaling as I used to do when it was smoke coming in and some of it going out.

Getting unhooked from cigarettes reminds you that your personal growth is a continuing thing.

Whether you be 70 or 17, what you do with your head, your thoughts about yourself and things, are ever-changing, evolving, broadening, wising up.

If the way that you are you, makes you unhappy about you, then change that part of you, that way about you. End that unhappiness about you.

If you are 70 years old and you've been unhappy about a part of you—the part that nags you to light a cigarette—then ignore that nagging, and change. That change will make you a happier you.

That's an emotional but thoughtful rock to hang on to. You have reasons to use both intangible and tangible pacifiers to get you past the times you used to suckle yourself on nicotine.

Weaning is rough.

But it is SO POSSIBLE if you cling to something, to somebody, to you-power, to a reminder that you're going to make it, like this book, which says you're going to make it.

Like the words you've written, or are going to write.

Communicate with you.

Touch that craving with words, words that recognize that the craving is there, that it is not bigger than you—and it will be less.

Use the words, the emotional, psychological, physical rocks and worry beads and pacifiers to help. You deserve something nice to happen to you today. Buy a little gem, a little semi-precious rock, or ask somebody you love to gift you with one, and then invest it with the power to give you solace and quietude.

And when you think, even for a moment that you're too weak to last without cigarettes, remember that JUST BECAUSE I WANT TO SMOKE DOESN'T MEAN I WILL.

Doing is a long way from wanting.

It's all right to want a cigarette. Admit that. Tell anybody and everybody that you want one but that you're going to manage without one.

That resolve of yours is a most precious gem to hold.

Some gems you can hang on to:

_____ a rock	_____ a gum ball
_____ a phoney cigarette	_____ a sea shell
_____ a pencil	_____ a semi-precious stone
_____ a worry bead	_____ a friend's hand
_____ a plastic cigarette filter	_____ Silly Putty

Way 14

Is Your Doctor Worthy of You?

Are you making the choice not to smoke partially because of what your doctor told you?

I used the word "partially" because I don't believe people choose not to smoke only because doctors say, "You must not." It still remains a matter of individual choice, motivation and determination. Your choice may be instigated or influenced by what a doctor says, but it's still you, all alone, who must make the choice. It's like being born or dying. You do it alone.

There are some helps. There's the doctor saying, "Don't." There's the kids or your relatives or statistics.

As we said earlier, this book never once *tells you to quit.* It says you're big enough *to make the choice,* it offers some helps, and it tells you about some of the rewards.

But doctors can be powerful in this problem-solving.

Many doctors don't realize what a serious depression a patient is thrown into when the patient happens to see the doctor lighting up.

The first time I happened on that scene really turned the rest of my day into a bummer, and me into a bummer of other people's cigarettes. Until I realized that "What the hell?" My doctor has hang-ups and weaknesses, too. I will not allow them to be dumped on me."

One way to use a doctor while you're learning not to smoke is to discuss a prescription for a tranquilizer, like Valium, or a mood-elevator, like Elavil.

You're already using them? Then talk to your doctor about the wisest way for you to go. Ask for something helpful in quieting the wanting for nicotine.

I was using Valium to help recovery from a medical problem when I first began kicking smoke. I learned that while Valium isn't the answer, it can help you to find your own answers by soothing the restlessness that is there when you want to light up but choose not to.

It is well to be a little bit afraid of tranquilizers in order that you do not transfer your addiction from nicotine to drugs. But, used wisely, tranquilizers may be helpful. Consider them a temporary help. It is so much easier to never need another Valium than it is to never need another cigarette!

If you are using a prescription medication to help you, be close in touch with your doctor. Your doctor knows, from personal experience probably, just exactly what you're going through and so can be extremely supportive while maintaining a strong hold on the refill-ability of your prescription.

At a six-day seminar, sponsored by the American Cancer Society for doctors and journalists, I saw that more doctors smoked than journalists. Those doctors, most knowledgeable in their field, didn't know much about themselves. They didn't know they had a choice. They didn't know they could let cigarettes go.

At a conference attended by 85 mind-expanding type doctors, psychiatrists, psychologists and behavior modifiers, 60 of them were smoking. Several members of the helping profession urged me to join them in a smoke even though I had not been "using" for several months. Another with greater love and wisdom said, "Our track record is lousy. Stay with yours."

Think about the people who might bear undue influence over you, who could make light of your determination, and figure out why. One day, you can help them.

Use blatantly those people who make you feel comfortable while they help; use cautiously the pills which help; use yourself—your you-power—even when it seems to be weak and waning. It's there and it will be stoked and replenished as you use it. Your own personal power is like mother's milk. Marvelously, if you use it, there will be more when it's needed. Using it just makes more.

The people who succeed at what they want to do had to decide they had the strength to make success. So do you. Make a list of the people who want you to succeed, who will even help you to succeed, the people whom you are happy-ing up by not lighting up. _____

_____

_____

_____

_____

_____

Now list the people who don't think much of your choice to become free of cigarettes, those whom you feel aren't really backing you. _____

_____

_____

With that list completed, you know whom to avoid as much as you can for the next few weeks or months.

Way 15

Words-Wise

If you're choosing to be free from cigarettes and are using this book as one of your aids, your feelings by now are mixed and many. As you face another night or another day without cigarettes, you are experiencing probably some happiness because you are trying, some anger because it's not easy, some love for yourself because you are such a marvelous achiever, some fear that you're going to blow your choice. Check the words that describe how you may feel about yourself in the next few days. If you expect these feelings, they won't be shocking enough to send you back to the pack.

You may know:

HATE

I feel:
- ☐ spiteful
- ☐ mean
- ☐ bitter
- ☐ unlikeable
- ☐ detestable
- ☐ worthless
- ☐ low
- ☐ odious
- ☐ rotten
- ☐ worthless
- ☐

FEAR

I have much:
- ☐ concern
- ☐ worry
- ☐ anxiety
- ☐ dread
- ☐ nightmares
- ☐ daymares
- ☐ terror
- ☐ fright
- ☐ harassment
- ☐ misgivings
- ☐ cold sweats

ANGER

I am:

☐ hostile
☐ resentful
☐ vexed
☐ up-tight
☐ offended
☐ sore
☐ displeased
☐ tormented
☐ mad
☐ pissed

HAPPINESS

I am:

☐ high
☐ joyful
☐ lucky
☐ delighted
☐ glad
☐ giggly
☐ pleased
☐ smiling
☐ groovy
☐ merry
☐ light-hearted
☐ marvelous

LOVE
I feel:

☐ likeable
☐ tender
☐ endearing
☐ fond
☐ affectionate
☐ amorous
☐ huggable
☐ comfortable
☐ comforting
☐ sexy
☐ secure
☐ glowing
☐ warm

DISAPPOINTMENT
I feel:

☐ frustrated
☐ tense
☐ deluded
☐ rejected
☐ bummed-out
☐ hurt
☐ inadequate
☐ failed
☐ harsh
☐ unsatisfied
☐ shocked
☐ miserable
☐ unhappy

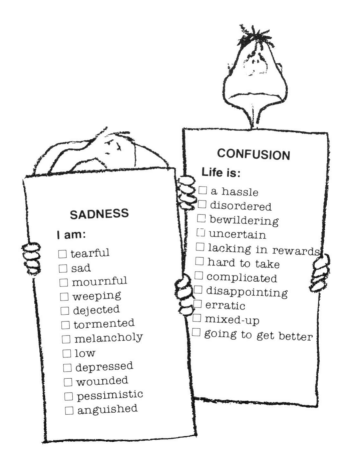

SADNESS

I am:

☐ tearful
☐ sad
☐ mournful
☐ weeping
☐ dejected
☐ tormented
☐ melancholy
☐ low
☐ depressed
☐ wounded
☐ pessimistic
☐ anguished

CONFUSION

Life is:

☐ a hassle
☐ disordered
☐ bewildering
☐ uncertain
☐ lacking in rewards
☐ hard to take
☐ complicated
☐ disappointing
☐ erratic
☐ mixed-up
☐ going to get better

Way 16

The Delicate Balance:
Wait, Wait for the Crisis to Pass

You are being engulfed suddenly and excruciatingly by the desire to have a cigarette. You ask yourself, "Why not?" and you answer: "Because I choose not to."

That won't be the end of it, you know. A crisis, a need to smoke, hits you and hammers you and says, "You will go get one and light it." It insists you will pick from a package a cigarette to pop into its rightful place—between your lips. It directs you to reach into your friend's pocket to help yourself to a cigarette for sanity's sake. It sends you running from your apartment or house to beat on a neighbor's door to borrow a cigarette. If you are a more private person, you will feel like turning the house over on its attic in your search for a cigarette.

The need-crisis seems to be in command.

It is not.

You may think so; prove it isn't.

Try this.

Let the need for a cigarette engulf you, wash you over. You may feel like a little leaf caught up in a current of need. You swirl in it, are buffetted about by it, are reduced to tears or to pounding your fists on the walls.

Measure how much you can take.

Gauge it by another former hurt, by another abstinence you once experienced. What was it—a hunger for food, liquor, sex, love, companionship, reassurance, kindness?—measure it by what it was like to be without those things when you wanted them.

Remember that you survived those abstinences.

The world didn't stop spinning on its axis.

You got through, scarred and shaken, perhaps, but you got through it.

This, too, this need-crisis, will pass.

Expect it.

Know its look.

Wait it out.

It will subside.

It will leave you stronger. Each crisis builds a kind of scab over the part of you that screams for nicotine. Your suffering and subsequent strength will hush that scream, and eventually will stifle it.

You may dread the next need-crisis with terror, or you may courageously stalk it. You have the experience of surviving one, or ten, to comfort you, so: lo! you are strengthened, comforted, and a survivor.

The sieges become less like sieges.

They get easier to handle.

You may not win every one. Sometimes I blew it and blew smoke, real smoke when I reduced myself to less than I thought I was and had a cigarette. I was astonishingly disappointed in the cigarette—it wasn't as good as I'd thought it would be. I was disappointed, too, in me. I wasn't as much as I'd hoped to be. Even though a bootlegged cigarette tasted quite good, I couldn't wash from my mouth the rotten taste of its conquest over me.

Then I learned to wait out the next crisis, to wait for the siege to end. It does! Wait for the worst to be over, and then just coast.

I learned to stand back and look at my feelings, like I was a third party studying me and my crisis. I communicated with me. I talked to me until I touched control again.

Sometimes I'd go to a mirror. Do that. Find out that your eyes won't.look squarely at you while you light up. But they will look back at you merrily and proudly when you know you're worth something. If you think, if you know, that you are bigger and better than a stick of nicotine, you can look directly into those mirrors of your soul and smile for real.

You will remember that "just because you're not there yet doesn't mean you're never going to get there."

Think about what you felt during the last time the craving for a cigarette seemed to engulf you, and how you feel now that the crisis is passed. If you blew it, say so, but announce firmly to yourself that next time you will be stronger and will not give in.

If writing about handling a crisis is easy, if you want to express it all, then let the writing come. The pages in this book can be a sounding-board for your words and feelings. Use them, especially when people close to you are tired of hearing about how mean the moments are without cigarettes. Although people close to you may get weary of hearing about your battle before you have won it, use this book, my words, your words, as a refuge.

How it was today and tonight when the need for a cigarette seemed excruciating, when I wanted to be a cigarette's slave again-----

_____

_____

_____

_____

_____

_____

_____

_____

_____

I am too involved in that to learn to hate.

Of course, you could be learning not to smoke because you think cigarettes are disgusting, because you think that smoking is a rotten thing to do. Maybe you're learning not to smoke because you believe your smoke is an impoliteness, a crudeness hanging in everybody's air? We started smoking for various reasons; we are stopping smoking for various reasons.

But this I submit because the realization is helping me so much. I don't have to force myself to do TWO things at once—to not use cigarettes, to hate cigarettes.

That's too much of a load for me to carry, so I won't.

The bottom line is—*I have choices.* One is to smoke. Another is to not smoke. I can look at cigarettes, the open pack on the next desk, and not light one up. So can you. Like a friend who learned she is a diabetic said, "I can look at pecan pie which I love and not eat some. I am more important than pie."

You and I are more important than nicotine.

We cannot yet be lukewarm in our attitude about cigarettes, when wanting to put a lit one to our lips is a burning, consuming issue all day long, and half the night.

But as with a lover who done us wrong, we the heros or heroines of this piece, can look back bravely, and say "Hey, I'm somebody new. I don't need you (cigarettes)."

UMTYUMP FLAVORS

NICOTINE & CREAM	TOBACCO ROAD
HAVANA SPLIT	UPTA SNUFF
MARBLE ROW	CHOCOLATE MENTHOL
COPENHAGEN DIP	TURKISH DELIGHT
PALL MALT	CHARCOAL CHIP
PELL MELT	HOOKAH FLOAT
SMOKED SALMON	NICOTINE & TAR
GUADALAJARA GRASS	POT LUCK
KENTUCKY BLUE	NO VANILLA

WE HAVE FILTERED
STRAWS

HAND-
PACKED
CARTON

Way 17
Ad-Mire

Advertising's gambits today are wholesomeness and sensitivity. The man in the cigarette ad looks like a gentleman, but powerful for sure sexually and on the tennis courts. The woman in the ads looks like she'd just finished a bowl of granola, or a hike through the forest. She's in jeans, and he's in jeans. They imply Merit, real Kool, as they gaze at their Dawn or at a charcoal-recessed filter with the same look of awe one might reserve for the Second Coming.

They've got More, more than you and me. All 120 millimeters more. And they're proud people, too, the ad tells us, with their long and more cigarette which is, we learn, akin to being American, "as American as the Grand Canyon," "as American as the Redwoods." It is pure patriotism to buy and smoke cigarettes.

The ads formerly featured a hard he-man from a country way out west where a guy'd walk a mile for a smoke from his kind of pack. The woman the ads used to feature was a sultry, swankily-dressed female adorning a setting as artificially glamourous as she. Now we get the pastoral scene, pressure-free, pleasure-promised. With a titillating Eve. The inference is that there's a little or a lot of the seductive, svelty-triumphant Eve in all women who buy Eve.

I like the reassurance, as many women do, that we've come a long way, baby, maybe, haven't we? Up front now where it counts. Not behind the woodshed. Not in front of the kitchen range. But in an executive place. Where we're smoking Virginia Slims and are slim like Virginia.

And how gratifying to find refuge, like the one the adwriter's rationale provides in the Vantage ad which asks, "How many times have you decided to give up smoking?" The query is a grabber. We're drawn to it by the justification it gives us to smoke, to buy Vantage. We're justified because we enjoy smoking and because Vantage provides us that enjoyment with little risk, it says they're almost as harmless as Carlton. But then "nobody's lower than Carlton."

But there's no dilemma. Lark tells us there's no dilemma. The Lark ad says now we can all smoke and breathe easier because the tar and nicotine content in Lark is one we can hack. Unless you're a True smoker—True's 100 millimeter cigarette is lowest in tar and nicotine and the U.S. Government says so, says a True ad. The man in the Winston Lights' ad seems to sneer at that. Low numbers are one thing, but not everything, he says. How false his fable—"I smoke for one reason—taste." We know it's more than that. But the man in the ad who says that, the woman in the ad who says that, have the look we like, a look that says they're assertive, attractive, interesting, successful. Could it be that if we pick up their brand we'd pick up their brand of attractive, interesting assertive success?

Wouldn't it be good to be guilt-free, to say even on a Tuesday, "Thank God, it's Friday" because now we have a cigarette called TGIF. The inference is that we can enjoy the abandon of a work-free weekend every time we light up.

In one year the cigarette industry created 30 new brands of cigarettes, all 30 aimed and named to hit us where we are most vulnerable emotionally.

The cigarette industry spends more than one-half million dollars a day to convince us to keep on buying, to entice new buyers. For every 12-inch sign that says "no smoking" there's a slick magazine page or giant billboard with a kingsize figure announcing that when you find Dawn it's going to be a taste-triumph. It's going to be slender, and spirited, and satisfying. And five minutes longer.

That's how it would be, (read, how I would be) with Dawn. But what about Max? Max promises alluring, lean, delicious, long, thin richness.

I want to be slender, spirited, satisfying, alluring, lean, delicious, long, thin and rich and to have long, blond sun-streaked hair. Few women, or men, wouldn't want all or some of that—the *in* image.

The ads almost make you forget that a cigarette comes with the look. You have to stand back from the ad, stand back from the art and words if you want to unhook from the Svengali that is a cigarette.

So do that.

Step back and admire the ads for what they are—art.

Admire them as pop art of our day and recognize that their message—"our product will bring you the ultimate in womanhood, the ultimate in manhood"—is pure pap.

It's contrived to sell cigarettes, by first selling you an image.

When they sell and you succumb what you'll get is nicotine and tar, a sense of loss—loss of your choice to use or not to use, and a tarnished image of yourself.

But since we are surrounded by ads, use them as an ally. Bootleg a vicarious kick out of the ads. You don't have to turn quickly past the ads in the magazines. Read them, appreciate the skill, even brilliance that went into writing them and laying them out, admire the art that makes them memorable, and then refuse to be seduced by the message.

Recognize them for what they are—contracts completed by high-powered ad agencies for clients who want you to smoke. To persuade you, to entice you, they've created graphics, pictures, posters which could become a prized kind of period art. One day cigarette ads may be collector's items, like the pre-World War II Lucky Strike green that went to war is now prized memorabilia, like the soft-drink posters and trays, circa 1910, now so sought after.

What you should not give to the ads is the power to collect you as a continuing or new customer. Your you-power is stronger than some copywriter's suggestions.

Really, there's more at stake than changing your brand of toothpaste. Let the ads convince you to buy a ticket on that cruise, to stock your kitchen cupboards with that kind of soup, to have gorgeous hair by buying this shampoo.

This book you read now is not billboard size, its message isn't in every slick magazine, or reproduced in 8-column newspaper headings—like the ads from the ciggie biggies.

It's a miniscule voice, but it joins the powerful one within you, asking that you recognize that you have a choice—to succumb to the ad industry's clout, or to save yourself from it, to buy or to walk on by.

It might be interesting to keep some kind of score—how many times lately have you been aware of a cigarette ad on a

_____ Billboard	_____ Matchbook cover
_____ Magazine	_____ Menu
_____ Newspaper	_____ Your friend's purse
_____ A friend's shirt pocket	_____ Grocery ad

Though they came at you, persistently, consistently, artistically, cleverly—they did not conquer!

Way 18
Discover What Works for You

There are bases that you have yet to touch. They are touchstones that are supportive when you need support, distracting when you need distraction, strengthening when you are wrung weak with wanting. Better than all of the above, perhaps, is that some of these ways provide you with new friends, a gallery of new friends, who want you to win and insist you will win even when you think winning is too far away.

The stop-smoking groups I'm thinking of are those fostered by the American Heart Association, the American Cancer Society, the Lung Association, the YWCA, the YMCA, the Seventh-Day Adventist Church, your church, your school district, the public health education agency in your community.

I wish I knew your community. Do you live in a lovely hamlet, population 139, or do you live in an exciting megalopolis with two million other people?

If I knew your community I might help you find the groups, the aids, the supports. Maybe we'd discover there aren't any. No matter. You can build you own aids.

Maybe we'd learn there are stop-smoking clinics and groups in session at various times but that you can't get to them because of your work, because of a transportation problem, because of your family responsibilities. No matter. It's handy to have help, but not essential—*you can unlearn smoking alone.*

I know dozens of people who have learned not to smoke without the help of a group or clinic. Just a few had rough drafts of this book and encouraged me to un-rough it and get it printed. They said it had helped them.

I know some people who put up as much as $500 to unlearn smoking at aversion therapy clinics.

We know that hundreds of thousands of people have unlearned smoking with the help of the American Cancer Society, the Heart Association, their church, their school district, their public health agency, etc.

There are other kinds of helps. Some more unusual than what your local tax-supported bureaus offer.

Is there in your community a group that meets to develop assertiveness? You can take charge of your life by learning to be assertive. What more marvelous manifestation of your assertiveness than to stop smoking?

Assertiveness involves exercising personal rights without denying the rights of others and without undue anxiety or guilt. Its development has much to do with making choices. My friends, Bob and Mike, non-smokers ,say, "You have a perfect right to smoke or not to smoke."The decision is yours. When you blame your smoking on someone else, something else, you're giving your control of self away. Take charge. Stand up, and assert yourself!

Is there near you a group which gathers to meditate? to teach meditation? to encourage meditation? The meditators I know don't smoke. Coincidence? It could be, but some of my meditative friends tell me they were able to let cigarettes go—to just let them go easily and peacefully—after they learned to meditate.

Transactional analysis is a powerful tool to have, perhaps because as one TA teacher, Larry Trettin, said, "You learn what you get out of smoking and, learning that, you don't need to anymore. The key is deciding to take up a new way of treating yourself (instead of tricking yourself). My experience is that contracts to *give up* something don't work. Contracts to *take up* a new way of treating yourself do work."

There are encounter groups, charismatic groups, there is est (Erhard training seminars).

Are they near where you live?

If any of them are there, don't decide that you don't belong in any of them.

You won't know until you get there.

I'm not encouraging you to join everything in town. I am saying that it's good to have the support of people who are where you are in learning not to smoke. Nobody understands an addict as deeply as another addict.

What I'm saying is—find out what works for you.

If clinics and groups and classes are available, visit them; choose the one that fits you.

If there are no such organizations in your community, or if you can't get to them, use this book and its positive statement: the power of your choice is stronger than any other kind of help in learning to be free from cigarettes.

If you want to be free, you can be.

The aids you discover for yourself will work best for you, because they are inimitably yours.

You can arrange to help yourself to hypnosis. It can be such a powerful ally.

Don't be dismayed by it even though the very word— hypnosis—conjures up people making asses of themselves as victims of night-club hypnotists.

Hypnosis does not create an unconscious stupor. Hypnosis does not mean helplessness. Hypnosis means development of mental calmness. It allows you to filter out negative thinking.

As my friend, hypnotist Ina Zell says, over and over, "Hypnosis is simply another state of consciousness in which we are susceptible to suggestions."

83

We are in light hypnotic states many times during the day, while we're daydreaming, concentrating, watching television, or relaxing and shutting out the world.

Use this kind of hypnosis to help you unlearn smoking. If there is a good practitioner near you, like Ina, plan and pay for some sessions. The cost of your smoking is inestimable. The cost of hypnosis can be budgeted. Have the practitioner explain to you what happens when you are hypnotized. Learn that you will not become some kind of zombie, that you will not do things against your own standard of conduct.

Hypnosis is suggestion.

The suggestion you'll hear is that you can let go of cigarettes. It's the same suggestion you've been giving yourself.

You already have been practicing a light kind of self-hypnosis.

There are books you can buy to teach you to become even more skilled at self-hypnosis. Invest in one, read, learn. If you cannot get the help of a professional practitioner of hypnosis, arrange a session with yourself.

Find a quiet place, set fire to some incense, light some candles, be comfortable, be warm, sit back or lie back and close your eyes.

Talk to yourself silently with all your consciousness riveted on the refrain you choose.

Some of the "talk" I make with myself goes like this:

"I am so happy with me because I choose not to smoke. I am so happy with me. I choose not to smoke. I am so happy with me."

Dare to smile at yourself while you're saying this. Relax and like yourself as you sit there congratulating yourself on your new happiness, even though just moments ago all of you was screaming for a cigarette. Concentrate on one picture—the picture of you sitting tranquilly and relaxed and in command, WITHOUT A CIGARETTE in your hand or near by in an ashtray. Focus on that picture, on that thought, and recognize how very much you will like yourself when you have won this hassle with nicotine.

Tell yourself over and over again, "I don't need that junk in my lungs. I don't need that junk in my lungs. I don't need that junk. I need my lungs. I need my lungs."

A favorite of mine is, "One day I won't even want a cigarette. Maybe that day is tomorrow. Maybe that day is tomorrow. Maybe tomorrow is the day I won't want a cigarette."

I know that if I believe this today there truly will be a tomorrow when it's true.

Or try: "I like me. Cigarettes don't like me. I like me. Cigarettes don't like me." Concentrate on these statements. Say them aloud.

Create some statements of your own, all your own, and probably better for you than any others because they are your own: _____

_____ I CHOOSE NOT TO SMOKE TODAY

_____

_____

_____

_____

_____

_____

_____

_____

_____

_____

_____

_____

_____

_____

_____

_____

_____

_____

A hypnotist taught me another ploy, so simple it would seem worth nothing, yet so relaxing it clears your mind of all distractions. It may help you get to sleep when you can't seem to get to sleep without a cigarette. Try this.

Lie back, close your eyes, breathe deeply and steadily, and count the number of times you exhale.

Counting exhalations induces paradoxical exhilaration and quietude. Every exhalation means a healing process is happening inside your lungs. Every exhalation means your determination to be free from nicotine is stronger.

Every exhalation means you moved one breath closer to not hurting so badly, so tell yourself, "This breath is for my victory, my liberation, for building my own sense of worth. This breath is for by own freedom from the pack, the match, the nicotine. . . . ."

Way 19
Weight for the Reckoning

Decide the same day you first choose not to smoke that you will not put 20 or 30 pounds of weight on that frame of yours.

For too long, both you and I used the fear-of-getting-fat factor as legitimate justification for continuing to smoke. Hadn't we seen what happened to the Porters and to Charlie when they decided not to smoke? They became balloons, full of pious hot air and righteousness about, "What's a few pounds matter when we have quit using those wicked cigarettes?"

Well, a few pounds matter. Matter a hell of a lot to me. I have never felt very attractive, but I have prided myself on maintaining a rather good figure. It hurt badly to see that while I didn't gain 30 pounds, I did gain eight or ten while I learned not to smoke.

It wasn't that I gorged on desserts to have something to do after a meal. It wasn't that I ate candy bars and doughnuts relentlessly to reward me for not smoking.

I believe there's a physical rebellion, a bodily protest when nicotine is withdrawn suddenly or slowly from a body which has used it and loved it and craved it for years.

Without cigarettes we feel deprived emotionally, psychologically, and physically. The physical dependence of the body on nicotine is as hard to break as our thought-process which touts, "Light up just one. It will make your mind and heart and soul all feel better." It won't. That's a bad tip.

But we who are choosing not to smoke are fighting more than one fight. I don't recognize them all. Even the experts disagree on whether nicotine is addicting or not. I insist that it is. As an expert user for 30 years, and as a reluctant non-user for awhile, I think I am qualified to say that withdrawing nicotine from the bodily system plays havoc with normal weight maintenance.

What's happening to you emotionally isn't any blessing, either. Just when you've been stroked lovingly by a child or friend who says, "I'm so proud of you for not using cigarettes any more!" there comes this terrible number on the scales.

It's enough to send you scrambling for a cigarette.

This whole nation is so damn weight-conscious. It's obsessively weighted down with thinness. Of course, the whole nation won't, but some of your best friends (?) might say deprecatingly, "Putting on a little weight there, aren't you, since you quit cigarettes?" You may have to look him or her squarely in the eye and say, "Yup, it's part of my growing up."

Then remind yourself that as soon as you can stop hurting from this choice, you'll worry about your weight, if it is a problem. It doesn't have to be. Maybe you're one of the strong-willed ones who can learn not to smoke and work out at a gym at the same time, or go on a food diet and a nicotine-free diet at the same time. I didn't have the power or the strength, or the time.

But somewhere in the new cigarette-less me, I learned that I could also say "no" to a lot of desserts and fattening foods. Maybe the admiring glances you will get when you say "no" to cake and candy will let everybody know that chocolate-power is less than you-power.

In the meantime, if there is more of you to love, don't let it unnerve you, deter you, while you are learning not to use nicotine. If you find that food helps calm the jitters, chew on something. Keep your mouth full. Keep your mind full of good positive thoughts.

And believe that you will level off at your usual weight when your body adjusts to being unhooked, because you will.

So for now treat yourself to an occasional banana split. Go make fudge with a friend and eat it all.

Be good to you.

All of you.

If your weight is a monumental worry to you, scale its size to a proportion you can handle by realizing that

_____ I don't have to weigh myself.

_____ I know I am gaining.

_____ I can't and won't worry about it now.

_____ I haven't gained the 30 pounds I thought I would.

_____ I haven't ballooned in size.

_____ I have not had to buy clothes three sizes larger.

_____ I have had to buy a few things bigger.

_____ I seem to be keeping my normal weight.

_____ Some of the new activities I've taken up since I began to learn not to smoke are slimming.

_____ I've learned that since I am in control and am learning to stop smoking I can use that control to say "no" to food I don't need.

Way 20
Save Yourself from You

Expect that you will try to sabotage your own quest for freedom. Sometimes obviously, sometimes in more subtle ways, such as listening to people weaker than you.

They are the people who will give you unsolicited permission to smoke.

An aged neighbor may say, "I've smoked for 40 years, and it ain't hurt me none." A relative may say, "Quitting smoking is torture. I tried once and was miserable and you're miserable now. Here, have one of mine." The girl at the check-out stand says, "You can't correct now what you did to your lungs for 30 years so why sweat it?" The professional man (my near nemesis was a well-known psychologist-author) said, "You crave cigarettes, you need them. It is wrong to deny yourself any longer."

All four of these people nearly took from me a precious something—my choice. I am choosing not to smoke. You are choosing not to smoke. Your choice and determination are precious. I was and am still addicted to nicotine. I am not a user right now because I choose not to be. But it is mind-blowing to remember how close I've come to letting others destroy my determined choice.

No one can force me to not smoke.

No one can force me to smoke.

If ever the warning, printed on all cigarette packages, is changed to an endorsement: "The Surgeon General has determined that cigarette smoking is truly beneficial to your health," then maybe that will be the permission we need.

Until then, we cannot allow unthinking family members or friends who feel how we are hurting for a cigarette give us ersatz freedom to smoke.

They don't have that privilege.

Nobody can give you a license to smoke but you.

Nobody can free you but you.

Those who would convince you to stay hooked are trying to fatten their thin spirit and self-image with large bites of your determination and choice.

You have a right to wonder, "Who the hell do they think they are, they who would deny me my choice? That's mine."

These are some stories (for real) into which you may fit. I was or am in some of them, others I know wrote or are writing them in real life today. Can you find yourself in any of them?

● ● ●

You needed at least a "B" to qualify for your scholarship. You've just learned your grade is less. A classmate says, "That kind of news calls for a cigarette." Would you know two real disappointments that day if you succumbed and smoked?

● ● ●

Your family pet has been run over by a car. As neighbors gather to help you, one says, "You really need a cigarette to get you through this. You can start stopping again tomorrow." Imagine how it would be to have that much anxiety, and yet hear yourself saying, "No, thanks, I'll get by . . . . ."

● ● ●

You've landed the lead in the biggest dramatic production your community will see this year! You are excited, gratified, apprehensive, all at once. You need a cigarette. You deserve a cigarette for a celebration! But wouldn't you write your name in brighter lights if you continued in your strongest role—that of a non-smoker?

● ● ●

92

Everybody at the plant knew the promotion was going to be yours. Except management. The big job with bigger pay went to the new person. Wouldn't it help to cover your disappointment if you lit up and put some smoke between you and the sympathizers? Or would you look and feel better about yourself if you knew co-workers were saying, "Thought for sure that would set off a smoking binge but it didn't!"

• • •

Things are so humdrum. Life is a bowl of blah. Nothing exciting, even interesting, is happening any place in your life. Today is like yesterday and tomorrow will be just like it, hard to describe, because there is nothing different to say about it. You deserve to smoke if for no other reason than to add something. But you know deep down that smoking is a minus. Can you look about you for additions to your life that can be marked plus, maybe A-plus?

• • •

What you merely suspected is true. Your marriage partner is deeply involved with someone else. You feel a deep, deep wounding hurt. Cigarettes would help salve it, you think. Could you stand to lose both your trust in your partner and the progress you've made in stopping smoking?

• • •

The baby's got colic, the older child's got tantrums, the car's got a cracked block, the checking account's overdrawn, the savings account's dead, and your husband says, "Other wives manage and keep house better, too." Wouldn't this be the time to join the neighbors for coffee and cigarettes? If you didn't, you could say, "Well, the only way is up. I'm still not smoking . . . ."

• • •

It's been just a great day! Everybody in the family is happy, loves you and shows it. Today at work you were admired and complimented. You bought a new suit and like your look in it. You like you! So why not top it all off with a cigarette? Or three? Or just before you go to sleep tonight would you recognize that the day hasn't been a total success?

• • •

My progress:
I told _____ people today that I am learning to be free from
      cigarettes.
_____ were impressed.
_____ were indifferent.
_____ told me how they had tried and failed.
_____ told me how they had tried and succeeded.

_____ times today I was discouraged.

Nobody noticed today that I am choosing to be free _____.
I noticed. _____.
I care. _____.

I need to read again some chapters in this book _____.
WAY_____and WAY_____and WAY_____are helping me the
most.
I will try tomorrow to develop WAY_____and WAY_____in ways
that work for me.

_____ times today I was encouraged in my choice to stop
smoking.
_____ times today people who said I couldn't, congratulated
me.

I feel more positive about me and what I can accomplish _____.

Way 21
Hit at a Myth

There are more myths about "giving up" smoking than there are about sex.

Undo some of them.

Undo the one that claims you'll feel better physically because you have chosen not to smoke. You may not. If you expect to, and don't, that could be an easy out for you—"I thought I'd get rid of this cough if I quit smoking and I haven't, so why not smoke?"

Some people insist that they feel better since they made the choice. I didn't. I felt worse. All over, I felt worse. I never did have a cough, or trouble breathing while I smoked. It seemed then that nicotine gave me a lilt to my voice, a spring in my step, industriousness and the zest to work hard. I know the difference now. Cigarettes did none of those things for me, because now there's more lilt, spring, industry and zest in me without them.

But there is lethargy when first you begin to live without nicotine. It's damn wearying, to want and not have.

Getting over nicotine happens in stages, like grief, or joy, orgasm or disillusionment. The stage you expect first—that of feeling better physically—doesn't always happen FIRST. It happens later. I can't tell you how much later, because it's going to vary from you to me. You'll know it when you get there.

Another myth is that food always tastes better once you've chosen not to smoke. It may, it may not. It may taste the same. There'll be times you don't care about food. Only about cigarettes. Times when you'd trade your heaping plate of favorite foods for one lousy butt of a cigarette. I always have loved food. It always tasted good to me. At first I learned not to smoke, I learned to dislike the look of a meal because all I could think of was, "After this meal, there will not be a cigarette with my coffee, with my after-dinner drink, with nothing." So sometimes I skipped a meal. Didn't hurt.

Sometimes I extended a meal.

In a restaurant or at home, I extended it by eating another thing while other people smoked. Rarely was it dessert. Many times it was a finger food—celery or carrot sticks, Euphrates crackers, salami slices, pickle chips—anything that kept my hands busy and the calories down. If you've psyched yourself into enjoying other people's smoke, enjoy that and a pickle, but don't expect that food's going to taste better just because your taste buds aren't coated with nicotine.

It could be a game. Write down what you've always heard about learning not to smoke, then compare it to what's really happening. You can destroy the myth you fed yourself—the one about not having a choice. You do have a choice.

You are using it to get free. You are doing it! Tell somebody! Write it down. Rejoice, you myth-killer.

Hits or myths?

I thought of the times the craving for a cigarette would be stronger:

_____ when I woke up.
_____ with my first cup of coffee.
_____ when I got to work.
_____ when everyone left and I was alone.
_____ after an argument with my spouse.
_____ when I read the newspaper.
_____ while I watched television.
_____ when trying to make a decision.
_____ after dinner.
_____ just before I went to sleep.

_____ _____

_____ I was 100% right.
_____ I was 50% right.
_____ I was all wrong.

The cravings were strongest when:
_____ I was bored.
_____ I suffered a disappointment.
_____ I was faced with a new situation.
_____ I saw such small hope that I could win.
_____ I was depressed.
_____ I was scared.

I handled the cravings by:
_____ phoning a friend.
_____ yelling about how I wanted a cigarette.
_____ going for a walk.
_____ lighting matches and candles.
_____ finding some interesting food to eat.
_____ running on the beach.
_____ riding a bicycle.
_____ flying a kite.

Right now:
_____ I am so proud of me.
_____ I'd rather not say how I let the craving handle me.
_____ Ask me tomorrow.
_____ I DO feel better physically since I chose not to smoke.
_____ I DON'T feel better yet.
Some of the ways I feel better are:
_____ I cough less.
_____ I have fewer headaches.
_____ My complexion is better.
_____ My eyes are clearer.
_____ My chest feels lighter.
_____ I don't have as many sore throats.
_____ My bad breath is gone.
_____ I don't get winded during exercise.

_____ _____
_____ _____
_____ _____

_____ The date I began to feel better_____

Way 22
Get Back on Your Wagon

So you've fallen off your determination, gone on a cigarette binge? Made an ash of yourself? You got up in the middle of the night to have a cigarette, practically inhaled even the filters of forty of them on the job today, and smoked up a storm in a saloon after work?

So who's perfect? Who among us, the hard-hooked ones, hasn't blown it? Allow yourself the right to be imperfect.

Allow yourself the right to fall down while you're still learning to fly.

It doesn't mean that you can't get unhooked.

It just means that it isn't easy.

A teenage friend told me, when I was first beginning to try to live without nicotine, "Just because you're not there yet doesn't mean you're never going to get there."

He didn't know that just then I had no hope of getting there.

All of me was screaming for a cigarette. I was so burned up inside over not being able to burn a cigarette that my spirit and determination were both burned down.

It was so easy to say, "I'll never make it, so what the hell?" and to go to a drawer where I kept some cigarettes. There is a mirror over that drawer. I saw myself about to light another—and then another—and something stopped me.

I realized I was using my guilt about the smoking binge to fuel up and foul up the rest of my days. I was a singe-ed sinner, not strong enough to get unhooked, not worthwhile enough to stay that way. I was damaged goods.

Then I remembered that teenage friend—"Just because you're not there yet—" And I wondered what the new me would look like if I ever got there. And if I'd like me when I got there? I certainly didn't like me now.

I'd have to clean off the guilt and the self-recrimination, even if I still wanted a cigarette.

Even if I still wanted one, I didn't have to smoke one.

You can want to and not do.

If there's any one hard fact I learned from all this wailing, stupid travail is that YOU DON'T HAVE TO, JUST BECAUSE YOU WANT TO. Once I recognized that *wanting to* didn't mean I WOULD, I was much more comfortable in living without cigarettes. The WANTING gets lesser, too. It gets less persistent, less consistent in the degree that it hurts you. Eventually, the wanting is reduced to an annoyance, an infuriating annoyance at times, a merely annoying annoyance at others.

But not until you stand aside and look at you, recognize your inestimable worth, and use that worth to fight this thing.

You are courageous and beautiful because you want to get unhooked. you wouldn't have come this far in this little book if you didn't have the stuff it takes to put cigarettes down. For today? For tomorrow? Don't think about how you'll get through Christmas without them. Don't imagine suffering through a family crisis without them. Don't worry about going through next week without cigarettes. Find the situation you can say "yes" to. You can say, "Yes, I choose to be free."

You can promise yourself "Yes," I'll keep my promise to me because I'm worth a promise-keeping." Put all the tomorrows out of your mind. Today is all you want to handle. Today.

It takes a while to get well.

To teach thousands of taste buds that they don't need the taste of nicotine takes time. To teach a body, addicted psychologically and physically, that it doesn't have to have a "fix" every 15 minutes takes time.

To develop the surety that "I AM MORE IMPORTANT TO ME THAN CIGARETTES ARE TO ME"—that takes time.

100

Remember, just because you're not there yet doesn't mean you're never going to get there. The only person or power in the world that can keep you from getting there is YOU.

If this book doesn't help you to get free from cigarettes, I think it will fix it so that you will enjoy cigarettes less, that you will hesitate as you light the next one (if there is a next one), that you will look at a burning cigarette and wonder "*Is* it burning me down?" Like the drinker who's gone to a few meetings of Alcoholics Anonymous and finds it harder to enjoy a drink after an AA meeting.

Let's talk about "enjoy." I always said, "I enjoy smoking. I really enjoy it. I'm entitled to that enjoyment."

I dared anybody to deny me, my statements, my enjoyment.

What I had forgotten was the joy of not smoking.

Wow! there is joy in not needing.

There is almost ecstasy in the realization you'll one day have that, "I'm free!"

Now that's joy.

That freedom is what I had denied me for so long.

Find that freedom again.

You had it once.

You didn't always smoke.

Learn again what a joy the freedom is.

When you've got it, you'll be carrying around some brands you won't have to buy. They are called ACCOMPLISHMENT, CONQUEST, LIBERATION. You can't buy them. They are priceless.

And remember that you can say out loud,a lot of times, "I really want a cigarette, but I'm choosing not to have one."

Another line that practically lifted me to freedom is the one: "Just because I'm not there yet doesn't mean I won't get there."

And important to know and to say is: "Just because I want to smoke, doesn't mean I will smoke. I can want to and not give in to the wanting."

Of course, the words won't do it, the lines won't do it—unless you let them.

Help them to help you by sprinkling the places where you live with the winning words.

Way 23
Grow Money

In a glass jar—brandy-snifter, decanter, sugar bowl—drop the same amount of money you have been spending on cigarettes.

Keep it conspicuous.

Make obvious to yourself and others how much it costs to smoke.

Never think that it's too little.

If it's a 50¢, its a start, it's a lot.

I don't know anybody who chose not to smoke because it costs a lot to smoke.

We who are real smokers know that if the things cost a dollar a pack, we'd still buy 'em. Supporting a nicotine habit is expensive! It's a very good reason to choose not to smoke. It's like setting fire each year to $300.00 or $400.00 or $500.00.

But most of us rationalize with—"I spend less on clothes than she does, so I smoke" or "He has other expensive hobbies—mine is cigarettes."

Numbers have little appeal to some people.

It's hard to be high on practicality.

But if you are trying to save money for a special project or trip or gift, add to that project-money what you save by choosing not to smoke.

Luxuriate in seeing it grow, let your money jar decorate a prominent place.

Or maybe you'd like to carry it around wih you, maybe in a special leather pouch, maybe in your old cigarette case, to fondle when you'd rather have a cigarette?

If you're re-enshrining what you're saving in glass, use some greenery, some $5 bills, some silver. The silver and the green says to you concretely, "I've chosen not to set fire to this much money."

Sneer as you pass a cigarette machine which blatantly announces that one pack of its wares now costs three 25-cent pieces.

Smile inside over your conquest as the person in front of you in the grocer's check-out line forks over $10 for two cartons.

You may think, as I sometimes still do, that $10 would be a small price to pay for just one cigarette.

But there's that challenge to yourself, remember?

If you hold out, that glass jar, that leather pouch will be filled with money to buy something that for you will signify accomplishment and not defeat.

There is inside of you that quiet courage that says, "I will not burn up my money and my self-control. There's a way to control the way I spend my money. One way is by choosing not to smoke, by getting unhooked..."

Way 24
Love and Leave

In the complex process that is withdrawal from nicotine, I am learning that I cannot learn to hate cigarettes.

I am learning that I can learn not to use them.

But hate them?

I've loved, you've loved, using them for too long.

Right now it is enough to bear to not use.

Nowhere does it say we have to hate what we used to keep near us.

That's a big block of thought.

I want some validation for what I bought, in theory and practice, for so long. I can have that validation. I can like them and not light them and so can you.

Hating them, or trying to, would be repudiation of all we'd ever lit, and of ourselves, during the years or months we lit them. I am not about to carry that big bundle of guilt around. I loved them and used them while I wanted to. Now I can love them and learn to leave them. If I can, veteran and inveterate smoker that I am, so can you. There were, of course, the cigarettes that spoiled things and events—the track meet, the wedding reception, the hospital visit. Then there were the other times.

I love the remembrance of some cigarettes I smoked.

Like a favorite sweater, like a well-loved love. Good, then, but not for now. There are songs that drift back, like cigarette smoke, in bittersweet memory, songs like "I'll Be Seeing You" and "All The Things You Are" (what are your songs?), and their refrains in my head or heart are good or painful, like "The Way We Were." Like a cigarette's remembrance can be.

They tell me ("they" are those people who pride themselves on announcing they don't miss cigarettes at all) that I will reach a place where I hate the thought of a cigarette.

"They" tell me that I'll see smoking eventually for what they think it is—a "disgusting" thing to do, they tell me. Well, I'm not where they are in their thinking, and I don't know if I ever will be, or if I ever have to be, if you will be or have to be.

I have all I can do right now to learn not to smoke.

Way 25
Too Big to Buy

It was not until the first anniversary of his death that his parents could say it out loud.

For a whole year it was just too much of an agony to talk about.

Their son died because of a cigarette. Just one.

It was the one that smoldered in the davenport cushions after the party was over.

In upstairs bedrooms Will and his college roommates slept.

Their apartment was totally involved in flames when the firemen arrived. Will lived almost two weeks, able to talk to his parents for a time, and then he died as the doctors at the hospital burn-unit said he might. He was 20, bright and buoyant. He had everything going for him—including somebody's cigarette.

It wasn't the cigarette that he died from—it was carelessness, you say? We are both right. It was the lit cigarette that provided the spark that set off the apartment house fire. It was somebody's carelessness that allowed that cigarette's fire to be where it was.

The combination of cigarettes and carelessness is a national disaster in terms of money, and a tragedy bigger than money in the case of Will's family and all the families who have lost someone.

The costs beyond buying cigarettes?

Inestimable, said sources I sought in the medical, insurance, building, sanitation, automotive, and tax fields.

I don't like statistics, mainly because I don't expect to be one.

I can read that nine attendance prizes will be give for every ten people attending and know that I will be the tenth, the one who doesn't win a prize. I can read that the American family changes residence every four years and decide that's an irresponsible statement "cause we're never going to leave our dreamhouse in San Pedro," and the next month we're moving to Ventura. I can read that in a study of almost 40,000 people for ten years, twice as many smokers died as non-smokers and I'll conclude that whoever is doing the survey "did" the statistics to serve the survey's purpose.

Then I ran into cold cash.

My husband said, "Here's $50 we can save on your car insurance if you are not smoking."

Then he showed me the fire insurance policy on the house and the clause that said it would cost $15 less if I didn't smoke.

Sixty-five dollars is not enough to convince me to give up something I love, like smoking.

What it does, though, is convince me that some shrewd heads out there wouldn't be giving us a better deal on insurance if they weren't sure that dealing with non-smokers at lesser rates wasn't good business. Money talks.

My son, Mike, a fire department engineer and paramedic, tells me that nationally there were 107,200 building fires last year and a resultant 96 billion dollars worth of property loss.

Our agent from Farmers Insurance Group, which represents 32 companies, said that smokers are involved in twice as many car accidents as non-smokers. I argued that with him. On what basis I don't know, except that I don't want to believe my smoking is a roadway hazard.

"It is," he said, "because even if you take only a split second to light up, to dump the ashes, to butt the thing out, your eyes are not on the road during those split seconds and that's all that it takes. And what about the times you've knocked the lit end off and had to look for it while you drove?" asked George.

My neighbor, Ben, blamed his $115 drape-cleaning bill on cigarette smoke—his.

The women who work at the American Cancer Society offices in Ventura said that cigarette smoking cost 5 billion dollars last year in illness and death. "But then, who can figure the cost of death?" asked Bunnie and Linda.

I read somewhere about a man who has smoked for nine years and is now smoking a pack a day and is, therefore, burning up about 7,300 cigarettes a year, (about half of the number I'd burn up yearly.) This man is now 26 and staticians figure that he's smoked up 6.25 years of his life expectancy. They further compute, though, that if he learned today not to smoke, he could retrieve the expectancy of those years by the time he's 36. He could really enjoy his senior years if he invested in the stock market what he invested in cigarettes ($153.00 a year). Using the same kind of wisdom in investments which he used in learning not to smoke, he'd have $86,861 when he's 65, according to a computer's computations.

I can't buy all of that. There's bound to be some years when he makes lousy investments. I don't really have all-out faith in investments or computers or dollars or cents.

I trust what I can see and not see.

I can see Will's obituary. I wrote it. I can't see the way his family misses him. I can feel it. Their cost is too much to pay.

Continuing Words...
Be Human to Yourself

You are deserving of special kindnesses, sweet gentling, nice goodnesses as you find your way on this whole new way of life.

Among them is the right to announce frequently and emphatically that you think, goddammit, that you really HAVE to have a cigarette.

You are not walking on the walls. You are not splattered in lil' pieces on the ceiling. You are together even in these crisis times when you think you will go mad unless you light up.

You won't.

Besides, temporary insanity is far more acceptable these days than lighting up.

Find some humor in all this heavy stuff about a new you. Not smoking is a marvelously liberating thing to do. You can laugh at yourself occasionally as you learn to get unhooked from nicotine. Through tears, too, sometimes, but don't believe that it's going to be all grimness, either.

Each half-hour can be a congratulation, for time you conquered without nicotine.

At first, opening your eyes in the morning, or whenever you open your eyes, will be traumatic. With eyes open, you know you face a seemingly endless day without cigarettes.

How many crises will there be this day, crises you think you can't face without a cigarette?

Maybe every half-hour will be an achievement?

Celebrate it!

Inwardly, a personal congratulation, a small "Thank you, God, or Whomever", a toast at the water-cooler, a victory when you tell a co-worker, "Guess what! I haven't smoked today!"

The crises do pass, the times you think you'll go mad do lessen and get lighter.

They will be lesser and lighter if you EXPECT them.

Just when you think you can't bear it, you'll discover that you just DID. Write it down, write down how rotten it was, the excruciating wanting and not having. Write down how weary but triumphant you are. *Triumphant* is such a great word. Use it! Telephone or visit the real friend who supports you in your choice.

Each crisis time you surmount gives you strength for the next one. Unbelievable though it sounds now, there will be days when you'll think about cigarettes only six times and want one badly only twice a day. It will happen to you that way.

I know because it happened to me.

It didn't just happen.

I made it happen.

And so will you, so can you.

Until now I would not have believed that I'd have joyful days without nicotine. All things in my life went better without nicotine. In every family snapshot, posed or candid, I've got a cigarette going. They began and ended my days.

Now I write and revel about not having them!

I, who love them!

I astonish and please me! As you will astonish, please; and love yourself because you made a choice.

You will like you so good.

You will be able forevermore to point to this month, this year, as the time you took over command of you.

Notes

Notes

Notes

Notes

Notes

Notes

Notes

Notes

Notes

Notes

Notes

Notes

We hope you have enjoyed reading this book. For more books with "IMPACT" we invite you to order the following titles...

Serving Human Development Since 1970

YOUR PERFECT RIGHT
A Guide to Assertive Living [5th Edition]
by Robert E. Alberti, Ph.D. and
Michael L. Emmons, Ph.D.

THE assertiveness classic, now updated and completely rewritten. New chapters on assertive sexuality, assertiveness at work, goal-setting, and more. Expanded material on anger, relationships, anxiety management. Totally revised, this FIFTH EDITION has more than double the material of the original 1970 edition.
Softcover $7.95/Hardcover $11.95   Book No. 07-0

THE ASSERTIVE WOMAN
by Stanlee Phelps, M.S.W. and Nancy Austin, M.B.A.

Assertiveness (NOT aggressiveness!) training for women! The original book that applies assertiveness principles to all phases of a woman's life: individual, feminist, mother, student, lover. Full of examples, checklists and helpful procedures. Over 200,000 copies sold and still going strong!
Softcover $6.95   Book No. 21-6

REBUILDING
When Your Relationship Ends
by Bruce Fisher, Ed.D.

A book for those who are putting their lives back together after divorce or after other crises. Rebuilding includes aids for coping with the fifteen "building blocks" that mark the path to recovery: denial, loneliness, guilt, rejection, grief, anger, letting go, self concept, friendships, leftover love, trust, sexuality, responsibility, singleness and freedom.
Softcover $7.95   Book No. 30-5

THE COUPLE'S JOURNEY
Intimacy as a Path to Wholeness
by Susan M. Campbell, Ph.D.

"Coupling, like life, is a continually changing process." Dr. Campbell guides us on the five-stage path of growth traveled by every intimate relationship - romance, power struggle, stability, commitment and co-creation. Here is help in discovering new meaning in the often confusing process of living intimately with another person.
Softcover $7.95   Book No. 45-3

PLAYFAIR
Everybody's Guide to Non-Competitive Play
by Matt Weinstein, Ph.D. and Joel Goodman, Ed.D.

Now you can play games where EVERYONE wins! Sixty non-competitive games for large and small groups: adults, young adults, schools, children, families. Detailed descriptions with complete instructions for "play-leaders." A delightful book that takes play seriously and makes it a way of life, filled with playful photographs!
Softcover $9.95   Book No. 50-X

RATTLE FATIGUE: And You Thought You Were Busy Before You Had Children!
by Linda Lewis Griffith, M.A., M.F.C.C.

A real Mom-saver! Light-hearted advice and practical tips for mothers of up-to-3-year-olds: time management, child care, housework, stress, relaxation, self-assertion, setting priorities. Effective ways to make life with little munchkins manageable and fun. Packed with perspective, insight, and good humor.
Softcover $7.95   Book No. 44-5

NO MORE SECRETS
Protecting Your Child from Sexual Assault
by Caren Adams and Jennifer Fay

A supportive, conversational guide for parents who wish to teach their young children how to prevent sexual advances. Points out that most offenders are not strangers but relatives and "friends." This important resource encourages open discussion — "no secrets" — between parents and children. Dialogue, games and other tools to help parents instruct children. 3 and up
Softcover $4.95   Book No. 24-0

LIKING MYSELF
by Pat Palmer, Ed.D.
Illustrated by Betty Schondeck

A child-size introduction to concepts of feelings, self-esteem and assertiveness for youngsters 5-9. Delightful drawings help convey its message to young readers. Liking Myself is widely used by parents and teachers to help children learn and appreciate the good things about themselves, their feelings and their behavior.
Softcover $4.95: w/Teacher Guide $6.45   Book No. 41-0

THE MOUSE, THE MONSTER & ME!
Assertiveness for Young People
by Pat Palmer, Ed.D.

Assertiveness concepts for youngsters 8 and up explained in an entertaining way. Non-assertive "mice" and aggressive "monsters" offer young persons an opportunity to develop a sense of personal rights and responsibilities, to become appropriately assertive and to gain a greater sense of self-worth.
Softcover $4.95: w/Teacher Guide $6.45   Book No. 43-7

STRESSMAP: Finding Your Pressure Points
by Michele Haney,Ph.D. and Edmond Boenisch,Ph.D.

A personal guidebook for pinpointing sources of stress — and finding stress relief! Questionnaire "maps" help readers survey people, money, work, body, mind, and leisure stress areas. Worksheets permit an individualized plan for relief.
Softcover $7.95   Book No. 60-7

LEAD ON! The Complete Handbook For Group Leaders
by Leslie G. Lawson, Ph.D., Franklyn Donant, M.A. and John Lawson, Ed.D.

Comprehensive guide for leaders of volunteer groups. Twenty-four easy to follow chapters make it easy to lead. Describes essentials for novices and experienced leaders. Indispensable for leaders of youth clubs, church programs, and other "new volunteerism" organizations.
Softcover $7.95   Book No. 27-5

Please see following page for more books and information on how to order

...more books with *Impact* 🐚

BEYOND THE POWER STRUGGLE: Dealing With Conflict in Love and Work
by Susan M. Campbell, Ph.D.

Explores relationship issues from the viewpoint that "Differences are inevitable, but conflict and struggle are not." Helps expand perspectives on relationships in love and at work. Psychologist Campbell challenges us to see both sides of a conflict by seeing both sides of ourselves ("Power struggles **between** people generally mirror the power struggles **within** themselves.") A creative and thoughtful analysis, accompanied by specific exercises to help relationships grow.
Softcover $7.95   Book No. 46-1

NO IS NOT ENOUGH: Helping Teenagers Avoid Sexual Assault
by Caren Adams, Jennifer Fay and Jan Loreen-Martin

Guidebook for parents provides proven, realistic strategies to help teens avoid victimization: acquaintance rape, exploitation by adults, touching, influence of media, peer pressures. Includes a primer on **what** to say and **when**. Tells how to provide teens with information they need to recognize compromising situations and skills they need to resist pressure.
Softcover $6.95   Book No. 35-6

WORKING FOR PEACE: A Handbook of Practical Psychology And Other Tools
Neil Wollman, Ph.D., Editor

Thirty-five chapter collection of guidelines, ideas and suggestions for improving effectiveness of peace work activities, for individuals and groups. Written by psychologists and other experts in communication, speech, and political science.
Softcover $9.95   Book No. 37-2

MARITAL MYTHS: TWO DOZEN MISTAKEN BELIEFS THAT CAN RUIN A MARRIAGE (OR MAKE A BAD ONE WORSE)
by Arnold A. Lazarus, Ph.D.

Twenty dozen myths of marriage are exploded by a world-reknowned psychologist/marital therapist who has treated hundreds of relationships in over 25 years of practice. Full of practical examples and guidance for self-help readers who want to improve their own marriages.
Softcover $6.95   Book No. 51-8

COMMUNITY DREAMS: Ideas for Enriching Neighborhood and Community Life
by Bill Berkowitz, Ph.D.

A unique collection of ideas for enriching neighborhood and community life. Hundreds of fresh, practical suggestions on street life, transportation, housing, festivals, recreation, employment, beautification, families, traditions, skills, food, economic development, energy, health, agencies, support groups, parks, media, workplaces and much more.
Softcover $8.95   Book No. 29-1

WHAT DO I DO WHEN...? A Handbook for Parents and Other Beleaguered Adults
by Juliet V. Allen, M.A.

A parent's "hotline in a handbook." Ready-reference answers to over 50 childrearing dilemmas. Comprehensive, practical, commonsense solutions that **really work.** Short on theory, long on practical solutions to crying, fighting, bedwetting, car behavior, self-esteem, shyness, working parents, discipline, and much, much more.
Softcover $7.95   Book No. 23-2

TRUST YOURSELF — You Have The Power: A Holistic Handbook for Self-Reliance
by Tony Larsen, D. Min.

A holistic handbook for self-reliance. Dr. Larsen, teacher, counselor and Unitarian-Universalist minister, demonstrates how each of us has the power to handle our world. This can be done in a completely natural way and depends only upon the power which we already possess.
Softcover $7.95   Book No. 18-6

SHOPPER'S GUIDE TO THE MEDICAL MARKETPLACE
by Robert B. Keet, M.D., and Mary Nelson, M.S.

Answers to your health care questions, and a "map" for finding your way through the maze of physicians, hospitals, clinics, insurance, tests, medications, and other services in the "medical marketplace." Explains technology and procedures. Sample questionnaires and checklists help you get the information you need for good decision making.
Softcover $11.95   8" x 10"   Book No. 52-6

Impact Publishers' books are available at booksellers throughout the U.S.A. and in many other countries. If you are not able to find a title of interest at a nearby bookstore, we would be happy to fill your direct order. Please send us:
1 Complete name, address and zip code information.
2 The full title and book no.'s of the book(s) you want
3 The number of copies of each book
4 California residents add 6% sales tax
5 $1.25 shipping for the first book. .25 for each additional book

VISA or MasterCard are acceptable, be sure to include complete card number, expiration date, and your authorizing signature
Prices effective January 1987, and subject to change without notice.
Send your order to:

Impact 🐚 Publishers
POST OFFICE BOX 1094
SAN LUIS OBISPO, CALIFORNIA 93406
(805) 543-5911